Mark, plea

ONE MAN on a BIKE

Adventures on the Road From England to Greece and Back

RICHARD GEORGIOU

BANOVALLUM
BOOKS

Published in Great Britain in 2019

by Banovallum Books
an imprint of Mortons Books Ltd.
Media Centre
Morton Way
Horncastle LN9 6JR

www.mortonsbooks.co.uk

ISBN 978 1 911658 13 9

Typeset by Kelvin Clements

Printed and bound by Gutenberg Press, Malta

This book is dedicated to Hilda and her husband.

ONE MAN on a BIKE

Adventures on the Road From
England to Greece and Back

CONTENTS

7

ONE MAN on a BIKE

DAY ONE

Lost Already

I KNEW SOMETHING wasn't right when my GPS proudly announced: 'You have arrived at your destination.'

I'd told it to take me to Dijon but there I was in the middle of bloody nowhere. I got off the bike and removed my helmet.

'This is not right. This is definitely not right,' I mumbled to myself, as I looked around.

When I checked the GPS, I found to my horror that not only was I not in Dijon—I wasn't even in France! My directional ability has always been somewhat lacking but finding myself in the wrong country was bad even for me.

The day had started early. Woken from my slumber at two-thirty in the morning, I sat on the edge of my bed feeling tired and numb. I'd been waiting for this precise moment for coming on two years and found myself

11

disappointed that I didn't feel even one pang of excitement. As I brushed my teeth I looked up at my reflection in the mirror.

'You don't have to wash for a whole month,' I said, trying unsuccessfully to find some enthusiasm.

Outside the darkness was almost complete. The slight glow from the moon seemed to erase all colour from the front garden, making it look most uninviting. I made my way downstairs.

The kitchen was usually a warm and friendly place. With its large windows and archaic Aga it was, without doubt, the beating heart of the home; however, when lit only by moonlight it had an altogether more sinister feel. I switched on the small light above the Aga and filled up the kettle. As I waited for it to boil, I glanced over at my dog, Nelly. She was fast asleep and snoring loudly. The desire to lie down next to her and snuggle up was strong but it would have been unfair to wake her.

I filled the Thermos flask with strong black coffee and poured the rest into a cup. Doing my best not to wake my wife Flowie, I tip-toed into the living room where my leathers were waiting.

Being so tired, I felt every gram of my protective clobber. The combination of a heavyweight pair of Richa trousers, an enormously heavy vintage Belstaff jacket and my Daytona boots turned me from an eleven stone man into a half-ton Klingon.

I squeaked and creaked back to the kitchen, slurped my

coffee and opened the back door. As the warm, humid night air hit my face I at last felt the first spark of excitement. The distance between the house and my shed was no more than about 30ft but during that short walk I went from tired to bursting with anticipation.

I opened the shed door and switched on the light. There, standing proudly in front of me, was my Honda Transalp, fully serviced and loaded with all my kit. I put my hand on her tank.

'It's just you and me old girl,' I said, feeling the excitement surging through my body. 'We're only going on another bloody adventure!'

In my mind I spoke the words calmly and with wisdom that only comes with age; in reality, they came out like a schoolboy just about to go on his first date. Maintaining a British stiff upper lip wasn't high on my list of priorities. I opened the double doors and wheeled my trusty steed onto the driveway.

'Crikey, I don't need to ask who ate all the pies,' I said, as I struggled with the weight.

With everything ready, it was time to say goodbye to Flowie and Nelly. I snuck upstairs and opened the bedroom door.

'Don't crash, have a nice time and leave your life assurance details on your desk.'

I smiled and kissed her. Downstairs Nelly was still sleeping soundly. I got down on my hands and knees and kissed her nose.

'I'll see you in a month pumpkin,' I said, putting my hand on her paw.

I knew what I was about to undertake had its fair share of risk. For a brief moment, I gave my mind free rein to wander. *If you crash this could be the last time you see your dog. She'll think you've deserted her.* I snapped back to the present and was surprised to find a lump in my throat.

As I climbed aboard my bike, I thought about how lucky I was to have a life that allowed for such an adventure. I waved goodbye to my wife and, with a tap of the gear lever, my journey began.

'We're bloody doing it old girl!' I shouted. 'We're on our way to Greece!'

Passing our local pub, I allowed myself to be completely absorbed by euphoric feelings of freedom and excitement. These kinds of trips only come around a few times in a lifetime and, as far as I was concerned, I was the luckiest man in the world.

As I sped up and left the village behind, the warm night air turned cold and I soon questioned my choice of jacket. And that was all it took for the floodgates of the reservoir of worry to open and overwhelm me with doubt. *Did I pack my passport? What about my wallet? Have I got my bike documents? Am I going to bounce over a big pothole and smash my testicles on the petrol tank?* I was less than half a mile from home and already I was a nervous wreck. I thought about stopping but told myself that I had checked, double checked and triple checked all these items in the days leading up to now.

'You're your own worst enemy, Richard,' I said, shaking my head. 'Man up and get to Dover.'

Motorcycle travel is necessary for my mental health. The lack of a radio and the continuous drone of the passing wind is the perfect environment for my brain to wander around sorting out life's many problems, and hopefully producing order from the chaos that is my mind. Many of my thoughts seem to revolve around worthiness. *What makes me so special that I should be the one to experience such pleasures as motorcycle adventures?* It gets bashed around in my head whenever I find myself doing well or in a good position. It's funny though, I never ask these questions when I'm having a bad time—I accept it as deserved. Payback, perhaps, for being a lazy little git.

I arrived at Dover earlier than expected so had ample time to find my way through to the ferry. There wasn't much else on the road, so I slowed right down and carefully followed each and every sign. The first turn had my GPS all but having a nervous breakdown. Its dictatorial tone combined with its irritating persistence in telling me to 'MAKE A U-TURN!' made ignoring it an absolute pleasure. Deep down I knew it was only a computer, but I couldn't help but feel that by ignoring it I somehow held the upper hand. Despite the GPS, I arrived at the ticket booth without putting a foot wrong. I showed the lady my ticket and was told: 'Line eleven please sir.' I smiled, nodded like someone who knew what they were doing and rode off.

I soon worked it out and ended up at the front of an empty line. To my left were some cars and to my right a long line of trucks. As I got off my bike, I felt a slight twinge from my backside. I'd only covered about 60 miles and probably still had about 6,000 to do. I mentally logged this and tucked it away, refusing to think about it in any way.

Even though a single cigarette had not passed my lips for almost five years, my first thought after removing my helmet was of a cigarette. Smoking was not only an addiction for me but also a habit. Even though the addiction was long gone, the habit sometimes came back to haunt me.

I walked around the bike and checked that everything was tight. When I was happy, I just stood there in awe of such an incredible piece of machinery. As my eyes drifted over the words 'Sahara Desert' on the back of the panniers, I was taken back to 2009 in southern Morocco. The evening was quickly approaching, and a fierce wind was erasing what was left of the already narrow road I was on. With visibility no more than about 20ft, I had no choice but to keep my speed right down, reducing airflow to the radiator to almost zero. This, combined with the fact that the air temperature was in the high forties, meant the bike was running pretty damned hot. On top of that, the air filter was almost completely coated in sand and suffocating the poor girl—yet she never missed a beat.

Daydreaming about the incredible resilience of the Honda Transalp, I heard a familiar sound. I turned around to see another Transalp stop behind me. Introductions were made and we talked excitedly about our prospective trips.

Soon we were ushered onto the ferry. One of the great things about travelling by motorbike is that you're different, which really means that you're being watched by lots of people most of the time. This is great when you're being ultra-cool and everything is going according to plan but when you're wobbling away on a heavy bike, on which you can't touch the ground, it's not so great. In full sight of the car drivers, foot passengers and truckers I rode up the metal ramp. A chap dressed in a headache-yellow all-in-one pointed to my parking space for the trip and told me to put my front wheel into the contraption. I got it right first time without dropping it. I was the god of cool, though I had no doubt I would make up for it by being a complete idiot at some point in the future.

I watched the cars enter as the chap in the all-in-one strapped my bike to the floor. It was always the same procedure. They'd drive onto the ferry, get out, press a button to lock their cars and make their way upstairs accompanied only by a small handbag or wallet. My set of procedures were far more arduous. I had to put a padlock onto the front and back of each pannier, unplug the electrical connections from my tank bag to the motorbike and remove it from the bike. Then, while dressed in my thick, heavy leathers, I'd have to grab my tank bag and crash helmet and stagger up three flights of stairs to the seating area.

Upstairs I found a seat and took up residence. I watched everything going on and thought about the month ahead. It wasn't long before my eyes became heavy and I drifted off to sleep.

I was woken by a large metallic clang that seemed to resonate right through the heart of the ship. This killed all conversation and for a moment it seemed as if everyone held their breath. My mind is a funny thing. The moment there's an opportunity to make a complete idiot of myself it seems to jump up and volunteer. In the silence, I heard my mouth open and loudly say: 'Who killed Kenny?'

No one laughed, least of all me. I sunk a little lower in my seat and closed my eyes again. Slowly the chatter and background noise returned, and I slipped back to sleep.

I can't have been asleep for more than a few minutes before the ferry started moving. The engine note changed, and the ceiling lights started clattering as they danced around in their fittings. A cup of tea on the table next to mine was jiggling closer and closer to the edge. I watched silently as it approached the edge, then fell onto the floor. It didn't break but spilt its contents all over a lady's foot. With all the noise I didn't catch what she said but going by the look she gave her husband, it was probably for the best. He got up without saying a word and walked off. Just in case the lady looked over at me, I closed my eyes and pretended to be dead.

I was hoping I would be able to ask someone nearby to look after my stuff while I went to the cafeteria to see about breakfast but 20 minutes later the husband hadn't returned. I glanced at the lady, but she still had an air of violence about her, so I decided not to ask. It was probably a good idea to wait and have breakfast in France anyway.

After about half an hour I spotted the chap with the Transalp sitting on the other side of the room, so I upped sticks and lugged my stuff over to his table. We talked about our intentions and places we'd been. He said he liked to travel alone as he likes to ride slowly for long distances, which I completely understood. I lost the piece of paper with his name on, but I do remember he was going to Spain via some wonderfully wiggly route.

Before I knew it, we'd docked in Calais. The overhead speakers announced something unintelligible, so I waited patiently for the English version, which was equally unintelligible, so I gave up and followed the crowd. We stood at the top of the stairs looking at each other while pretending not to look at each other until the barrier was removed, allowing us to descend to the nether regions of the ferry. I noticed how most people looked fresh and ready for their day ahead. They smiled and chatted easily as I struggled down each step in my boots and leathers with my heavy tank bag and crash helmet.

By the time I reached my deck I was covered in a fresh layer of sweaty stink and irritated to high heaven by all the happy, shiny people with their smiles, lightweight clothing and ultra-white teeth.

When I finally reached my bike, I realised I was actually at the back of the ferry and was going to be the last to depart. This was fine with me as being the first off normally meant I'd be followed and laughed at when I turned the wrong way just seconds after leaving the ferry.

I had loads of time to get ready but for some reason I always feel the need to hurry. It's such a powerful feeling that I have to really concentrate to stop myself from panicking. I forced myself to relax and take my time but whatever I tried, I just couldn't shake off the feeling. This was something I needed to think about once I got underway.

I sat there ready to go for the next ten minutes until the car in front started moving. This prompted more feelings of needing to hurry, which I didn't appreciate at all.

'Oh, bugger off. I'll go when I'm ready,' I muttered into my helmet, safe in the knowledge that no one could hear me.

As I rode off the ferry and into France, I smiled. It was only a small achievement, but it was also the first which made it feel special. After a few minutes I stopped and typed Dijon into the GPS. With the destination set and the sky blue above, the world was my oyster. I pulled out onto the right side of the road and accelerated hard, quickly getting up to speed.

'That's country number one old girl. Dijon here we come!' I said, patting the side of the Transalp's petrol tank with affection.

The beautiful countryside kept my attention for a while but before long, my mind wandered. *Why do I always feel the need to hurry when leaving a ferry?* After some seriously deep thinking, I came up with an answer that seemed to make sense.

'Perhaps it's because I think of myself as inferior,' I said out loud, wondering if I'd hit the mark or not.

The thought that I would hold up people behind me or inconvenience the crew by not being ready to move when asked was absolutely out of the question. *So, this must mean that I value other people's needs as more important than mine.* Turned around, this means I value my needs as less important and so I must consider myself as less important. This was a theory that needed some more work, so I made a mental note to return and discuss.

'Take the third exit at the roundabout,' said the GPS, in its dictatorial tone.

I obeyed and looked around. I'd ridden from Calais to Dijon a few times before, so was surprised to find that I didn't recognise anything. Even the place names on the signs didn't ring any bells. 'Oh well,' I thought, 'I've never had much of a memory.'

It wasn't long before I started thinking about food and coffee. I kept my eyes peeled and pulled in at the first supermarket I came across. I parked up and set about going through the routine you have to go through when you're travelling alone on a motorcycle. I didn't mind at all as it was all still a novelty, but in the coming weeks I knew it would become tiresome. I removed my gloves and crash helmet, unzipped my jacket and unplugged all the cables between my tank bag and the motorbike. I then unclipped the GPS and put it in the tank bag, which was then pulled off the bike. I placed my gloves inside my helmet and checked the panniers were locked. Only then could I grab the tank bag with one hand, my helmet with the other and make my way into the supermarket.

In the large supermarkets, I'd use a trolley to make life a bit easier but being that this was one of the smaller ones that wasn't an option. As I wandered around looking for something that tickled my fancy, I squeezed between a shop assistant and the cheese counter. With my tank bag in one hand and crash helmet in the other it wasn't the most elegant piece of manoeuvring, but I made it through and continued on my way. I'd almost made it to the pastries when I became aware of something going on.

Behind me stood a lady aged around 40. She was slight of build and stood no taller than about 5ft. She had dark hair and a tanned complexion and was hopping along behind me trying to attract my attention. To my absolute horror, I saw that my magnetic tank bag had attached itself to her leg like a limpet and I'd pulled her along! I couldn't help but notice that her skirt had been pulled up by the tank bag and barely covered her dignity.

I'd love to tell you that I apologised in fluent French but the first thing that came to mind was: 'Oh shit, I'm so sorry.'

She looked at me and smiled, and then laughed. In

broken English, she said she'd had an accident when she was younger and had some kind of metal contraption in her knee and thigh. After a bit of careful tugging and a huge amount of embarrassment, my tank bag finally relinquished its vice-like grip on the lady's thigh. I apologised once more, made sure she was okay and left with a very red face and without having bought a thing.

'Only me,' I mumbled, loading my stuff back onto the bike. 'Only you, Richard.'

After a few more miles under my belt I spotted a café and pulled in. It was coffee and cake time. I was able to park pretty much outside the front window so didn't feel the need to unpack everything. I unzipped my jacket and hung my helmet on my mirror. Even with the heavy jacket it felt good to be free of stuff and I walked in feeling happy and light on my feet. Inside, I looked through the cakes and pastries.

'Such a fine selection, but what to have?' I asked aloud.

I looked up to find a lady staring at me as if I was some kind of madman. It was time to amaze her with my French.

'Er, excusez moi s'il vous plait.' The lady continued staring. 'Er, une tarte à la pomme de terre s'il vous plaît?'

I felt proud for almost a second until she burst into laughter. She poked the other lady behind the counter and repeated what I had said, and then they both laughed at me. I couldn't help but join in with the laughing and asked: 'What did I say?'

I'd ordered a potato tart, silly me. I pointed to the apple

tart I was after. The lady handed it to me and said: 'Tarte aux pommes, not tarte aux pommes de terre.'

'Aaah, merci beaucoup,' I put my finger to my temple. 'Imbecile.'

After my rubbish attempt at ordering food, I almost switched to English to order coffee but decided against it. I was in France after all, and it seemed only right to try to speak French whenever I could. It felt more respectful.

'Un grand café noir s'il vous plait,' I said, hoping I got it right.

'Tres bien, merci,' she replied, handing me a tiny packet of coffee.

After paying, I took my apple tart and tiny packet to the machine and made a small but perfect cup of coffee. Just as I was leaving, the lady shouted: 'Au revoir, imbécile!'

She was standing behind the counter with her finger to her temple and laughing. I laughed too and returned to my bike. As I stood eating, I looked around. I remember being in awe of the beautiful scenery and the open space the last time I'd ridden to Dijon, but this felt different. There were lots of people and buildings and it wasn't overly pretty. I glanced at the GPS. I was on the magenta line so must be going the right way.

'Don't worry old girl, just a bit further south and the roads will open up nicely,' I said, patting the side of the tank. 'I think we've taken a different route.'

As I rode off, I told myself to pay more attention to where I was going. I looked at a few passing signs, but my mind soon wandered. *What was this feeling of inferiority?* Before long I concluded it probably stemmed from experiences at primary school. None were overly bad, however they must have been sufficiently important for me to allocate them a little worth in my mind.

There's no getting away from the fact that I've never been the sharpest knife in the drawer and on top of that I'm also quite lazy. As a child at primary school the combination of these two attributes must have made me somewhat of a challenge to the average teacher. Most coped with me admirably but one, Ms Demon Teacher from Hell (not her real name), was simply abhorrent and boy was I scared of her.

I was left-handed, which upset Ms Demon Teacher from Hell, so I was forced to write with my right hand during her lessons. Then I was reprimanded for having messy handwriting.

'Just look at the state of your handwriting, Richard,' she'd say, frowning down on me like a worthless germ in a test tube. 'It's just not good enough. You'll have to do better than that.'

It was always a relief when I finally got sent to stand in the corner as I knew she'd stop hassling me. From that vantage point, I noticed she wasn't horrible to anyone else; it was just me. Everyone else seemed to be up to date with all their work. I, on the other hand, was behind in everything. I don't think it would be unreasonable of me to conclude that this was, in all likeliness, the beginning of these feelings of inferiority. Feeling inferior due to *being* inferior.

When I checked the GPS, it seemed I was making excellent progress. My rough calculations had me travelling for at least another two or three hours before reaching Dijon, but it seemed I was only 43 miles away.

'Well old girl, it seems we're doing incredibly well,' I said. A long pause. 'Surprisingly.'

As we made our way through those 43 miles, I couldn't help feeling a little disappointed as I watched the sights go by. Where were all those beautiful hanging baskets? And what about the open feel and super roads? When the GPS proudly announced 'you have arrived at your destination' I stopped and removed my helmet.

'This is not right. This is definitely not right,' I mumbled.

I opened my right pannier and removed a paper map and my Thermos. After pouring a nice cup of hot coffee, I checked the GPS.

'You have to be fucking joking!'

Not only was I not in Dijon, I wasn't even in France! Directional ability has always been somewhat lacking but finding myself in the wrong country was bad, even for me. Further investigation revealed that when I'd asked the GPS to take me to Dijon, instead of taking me to Dijon in France, it rather vindictively took me to a similarly named sweetshop in Belgium.

I looked up and found that I was indeed sitting right outside a sweetshop, and I was indeed in Belgium.

'Well, I suppose that explains why it doesn't look very French around here,' I said, feeling a little stupid. 'Because it's bloody Belgium!'

I laughed at my misfortune and slurped the rest of my coffee. Half of me found it funny while the other half wondered how long it was going to take to get to Dijon and how sore my backside was going to be when I got there. I re-programmed the GPS, very careful to select the town of Dijon in the country of France. I then checked the route, bit by bit, cross-referencing it with the paper map. I let out a big sigh when I realised how far I still had to go.

'You bloody idiot,' I said, staring at the screen.

A total of 289 miles to Dijon. Five hours and fifty-two minutes. With a heavy heart, I climbed aboard the bike.

'Sorry old girl, it seems we're not doing so well after all,' I said, patting the side of her petrol tank.

The reality of how slowly the miles ticked by came as a bit of a shock. The border with France didn't seem to be getting any closer and the drab scenery wasn't doing much for the soul. I forced my mind to conjure up images of wonderfully picturesque French villages with their colourful hanging baskets in full bloom, but it felt like Belgium was drawing me back, perhaps as some kind of evil punishment for not deliberately including it as a part of my trip.

Just as my mind began to wander, I opened my visor to itch my head and was been hit in the eye by something hard. Struggling to keep my eyes open and in pain, I pulled off the road. I removed my helmet and tried to look in the mirror but couldn't really see anything. After five minutes of poncing around and with one eye shut and the other closing in sympathy, I was starting to entertain the thought that I might not be able to continue my journey. I closed my eyes and sat there on the side of the road, dreading the inevitable. Then I removed a water bottle from my pannier, washed my fingers as best I could, took a deep breath and pulled my eyelid out as far as it would go, inserting my finger underneath and sliding it around. I instantly felt something and with a bit of work managed to get it out. It turned out to be a rather healthily sized black housefly.

Relieved, I blinked madly, allowing my eyes to water and clean themselves. Inside of a few minutes my eye was pretty much back to normal and I was raring to get back on the road. With my visor firmly in place I intelligently followed the magenta line on the GPS while keeping a close eye on my progress using the map in the top of my tank bag. It took me a little while to work out that the road I was on was called the E411 and the A4, then a few miles down the road, it changed, without rhyme nor reason, to the E25. Is life not confusing enough? Why would someone do that?

I concentrated on the route and before I knew it, I'd left Belgium and was riding through the Parc Naturel Régional de Lorraine. Wow, this was the France I was hoping for. It was spacious, beautiful and dotted along my route were picturesque little villages that melted the heart. After my detour into Belgium, this was just the tonic I needed.

As I admired the view from the discomfort of my seat, the miles slowly drifted past and I was in a world of my own, working through the woes of my life. Saying that my feelings of inferiority have been a contributing factor in my life would be to give them more credence than they deserve. Every once in a while, these feelings rear up and make themselves noticeable but even then, this has never really been a problem. Is it not all our little foibles that turn us into the people we become? *And who is this person I've become?* Luckily before I got the opportunity to start down that route, the GPS interrupted.

'Take the second exit at the roundabout.'

I did as I was told and recognised the place. To my surprise, I was only about 35 miles from Dijon. I pulled over and checked the map. I didn't fancy going through the middle of Dijon so made my way around the edge and looked for a campsite. I'd passed loads of signs during the day but now I actually wanted one they seemed to be rather thin on the ground. As the sun got lower, I had the familiar feeling of being up shit creek without a paddle. Then I found exactly what I was looking for.

I rode through the gate and up to a large sign that read 'Welcome!' in eight languages. The warm hue of sunlight made what was already a beautiful place look simply stunning. The reception was housed in an old wooden building with well-tended hanging baskets on each corner. A perfectly smooth roadway was edged with flowers of every colour and an open gate invited me in. There were enough people milling around to make it look alive but not crowded. I had arrived at a happy place and was 20 miles south of Dijon, in *France*.

At reception the sweet scent of flowers was replaced by what smelt like a glorious lamb stew with herbs and wine. Just what I fancied after my long day. A smiley lady filled out the check-in form with my passport details and took my money.

'You can park everywhere,' she said, gesturing to the whole place with a wide sweep of her arm.

I found the perfect spot, bumped my wheels up onto the beautiful green grass and parked up for the night. A wave of contentment washed over me. The late afternoon air still held its warmth from earlier in the day and a gentle breeze stopped the humidity from being oppressive. Some young children were playing happily outside their parents' tent and a small dog was running around and yapping at butterflies. It felt good to be moving around again. Riding the bike is wonderful but sitting still on that saddle for such long periods of time does me no good. My backside starts to ache after a couple of hours and towards the end of a long day, my knees make damned sure I know they're not happy.

I unpacked and checked my watch.

'Eighteen minutes. You're out of practice Richard,' I said, '...but you're a few years older.'

Normally I'd break out the stove for a coffee and food

but in my wisdom, I'd decided to take the Thermos instead and eat out on this trip. I sat on the ground in the entrance of my tent and poured a coffee, but it wasn't the same not having a stove bubbling away. Lesson learnt. I sipped and my eyes drifted to my notepad.

With a memory like mine, it's essential to write things down so I'd bought myself a pad and had written a basic daily plan. At the bottom of each day, I planned to write notes to remind myself of things that happened. Throughout the day I'd made various scribblings, which now made for some interesting reading! I smiled through some notes and cringed through others. If it continued like this, it was certainly going to be a trip to remember.

Coffee gone, it was time for a trip to reception to get some of that fine-smelling stew. The bounce in my step ended firmly when I found that reception was closed and deserted. I looked around for some kind of shop or bar, but the whole place seemed completely dead.

'Damn. I was looking forward to that.'

I briefly entertained the idea of a quick trip on the bike to for food, but time was ticking on and I was tired. The thought of sitting on that seat confirmed it was a bad idea. I pottered around for a bit, looked at the map and worked out how many miles I'd done. It turned out that I'd covered 458 miles (735km), not a bad result for one day but it would probably have been 100 miles less if I hadn't visited Belgium by accident. Silly me. I climbed into my tent and went to sleep.

DAY TWO

SUNDAY, 18TH JUNE 2017

A Grumpy Old Lady

AT ABOUT 1am, one of the children in the campsite started screaming. This started another child off, and then the dog joined in with some howling for good measure. I lay in my tent for a bit, waiting for it to stop but after a while decided my motorbike earplugs were a good idea. Duly inserted, from that point forward I slept like a baby.

I knew I'd had a good night's sleep even before I opened my eyes. It was one of those rare occasions where there is no waking process. You come around, and instantly you're completely awake. I unzipped my sleeping bag, stretched hard until my left calf cramped and checked my watch. It was 8am.

The inside of the tent was a good temperature and the sunlight made patterns on the walls as it shone through the trees, but it wasn't until I pulled out my earplugs that the world really came alive. I unzipped the door and glanced out.

The fresh morning air felt wonderful on my face. I took a deep breath and held it for a moment enjoying the feeling. I glanced up at the perfectly blue sky as I felt my lungs absorbing the oxygen from the inhaled air. The young children and the dog were far enough away that their noises were nothing more than pleasant background ambience. I sat there for a while absorbed in my surroundings but soon enough, my lust for coffee made itself known.

I screwed up my nose as I poured what was left from my Thermos into my cup. Even with its stainless steel innards, the coffee had a synthetic smell that made me long for the genuine article. I looked over the map and worked out a rough route for the day ahead.

'You did well yesterday,' I told myself. 'Today's route should be nice and easy. As long as you don't take a detour into Belgium, that is.'

I finished my coffee and with an inner contentment, set about packing up. I wondered if this trip was going to include experiences that would change my life, things that would improve me as a person or perhaps just times that would make me smile when I looked back from many years in the future. The anticipation of all these made the trip feel like a real little boy's adventure.

The combination of it being a Sunday morning, the beautiful weather and the fact that packing up was still a novelty made getting ready for the day ahead a pleasure.

My destination was a small town called Saint-Jean-en-Royans and getting there was to be a simple exercise of following the line on the GPS and enjoying the ride. With it being only around one hundred and ninety miles away I had time to take it easy.

Riding through the French countryside with my unzipped jacket flapping around in the wind was a wonderful experience. I kept my speed down, which kept the noise and turbulence to a minimum, and thoroughly enjoyed riding through a large chunk of the morning. After a couple of hours, it warmed up considerably and when I spotted a sprinkler watering a field, I found myself imagining riding through it. As I got closer it looked like Lady Luck was on my side and I was going to get a shower. To my amusement, I found that what I imagined to be a fine spray was more like a fireman's hose, and it was freezing cold!

After 20 minutes or so I was dry and meandering through the beautiful French countryside. With its fields of corn, edged with wild poppies and lavender, France was showing me her best and everything was fine with me except for, that is, a developing headache caused by a lack of caffeine. Before long I spotted a sign for McDonald's and decided it would be a great place to fill my Thermos with the wonders of fresh coffee. Being very careful to keep my tank bag away from everyone, I made my way inside. When I reached the front, I dazzled the teller lady with my brilliance.

'Six grand café noir s'il vous plait,' I said, feeling confident.

The response was far too complicated for my simple brain to understand but I noticed her tone went up at the end like a question. Assuming she was checking that I wanted six coffees I replied with: 'Oui s'il vous plait.' After a few minutes, I was served one coffee.

'No madam, six café,' I said.

'Six café?'

'Oui, six café.'

'Pour toi?'

Unfortunately, my French didn't stretch to 'I'd like six large, black coffees to fill up my Thermos please', so instead I got the flask out and waved it in the air. I pointed to it and said again: 'Six café s'il vous plait.'

When I saw the lady's face register that I did indeed want six large, black coffees, I felt relief. It soon turned to confusion when everyone behind the counter started chatting excitedly and laughing. Not having an iota of a clue as to what was going on, I just smiled and kept quiet. When I paid, the teller held up two fingers, indicating she'd only billed me for two. She smiled and I smiled back, said thanks and found a table.

I could see the McDonald's staff pointing and laughing as I filled my Thermos with the coffees but that was fine with me. My Thermos was full, and I had one left over which I sat and enjoyed immensely. I seem to have a knack for making people laugh. I used to think it was because I was funny but over the years, I've come to realise it's because I'm an idiot. As far as I'm concerned though, whatever the reason, making people laugh is a good thing.

With my caffeine addiction satiated I grabbed my stuff and returned to my bike. As I rode by, I could see all the staff's smiley faces. I waved and everyone waved back.

After a couple more hours on the road, I grew restless. As beautiful as France is, I craved more and found myself scanning the distant horizon for the first sign of mountains. When they finally came into view, I couldn't contain my excitement.

'Mountains!' I screamed, unable to come up with anything better. 'We've made it to the mountains!'

I patted my steed's tank, happy to be sharing such a wonderful moment with my faithful companion. Not long after, I found myself in yet another truly beautiful spot and pulled over. The absolute clarity of the air gave the colours a radiance like I'd never seen; it was as if nature had turned up the contrast. I switched off my engine and listened. The background noise was of water trickling along in the small stream that ran mostly parallel to the road. This was joined by the continuous sound of buzzing bees collecting pollen from the vast array of local flora. The small road meandered into the distance where the eye then met with the hugely impressive French Alps. To the left of the road was a stream and to the right was a small but perfectly formed cottage with a garden comprised of grass and flowers and a thriving vegetable patch. Nearby sat a light blue Citroen 2CV. Its owner, an elderly lady, pottered around with the car, removed some bags from the front and took them into the cottage.

I was absorbed by the perfection of the scene and decided I must capture the moment. I removed my camera from my tank bag and raised it to my eye, ensuring the composition captured the feel of the place. It was at this precise moment that the shouting started. I have no idea what the elderly lady was saying but it certainly wasn't 'Please, go ahead, take my picture.' After being absorbed by the nirvana of the last few minutes, it took my brain a few seconds to catch up with the new situation. I stood there, too stunned to move. When she started marching towards me with her walking stick raised above her head, I decided to stick my tail firmly between my legs and run away. Crikey. Old ladies eh?

I accelerated hard to escape and all too soon, adrenaline kicked in and I found myself zooming around the incredible mountain roads having a thoroughly enjoyable time. The short straights and hairpin bends had me throwing the old girl around like an agile little sports bike. With the previous episode fresh in my mind and the sight of the ever-growing mountains ahead, I revelled in my adventure. Yep, I was in motorbike heaven.

After a few minutes of fun, I returned to my normal sedate riding style and putt-putted into Saint-Jean-en-Royans. The day was still reasonably young, so I felt no pressure to find a campsite immediately. Instead, I rode around the town and found a nice little pub with a rather rowdy bunch of bikers occupying the car park.

'Perfect,' I said into my helmet. 'Fellow bikers to talk to.'

I rode through the only gap there was and over to the far end. When I dismounted, I removed my helmet and glanced at the bikers. They stared back with expressions of utter contempt and continued with their conversations. Quite often my first impression can be completely wrong so as I walked past them, I nodded and said a rather manly 'Hi.'

This didn't produce the result I was hoping for. Instead, they made it absolutely clear they were not there for conversation and promptly ignored me.

'Fuck you then,' I said, loud enough to feel manly but quiet enough to not be heard. 'Your loss.'

I bought a Diet Coke and gently lowered myself into a seat by a window overlooking the car park. The grumpy bikers looked very stressed as they studied their maps, waving their hands and frowning. Then without further delay, they mounted up and disappeared, leaving a peaceful silence in their wake.

My mind wandered to thinking about my own method of travel. Each day I have a start and an end point. Obviously, the start point is fixed but the end point is advisory and something to aim the GPS at. How I get there is reasonably unimportant. As long as my wanderings are roughly in the right direction, I'm happy. Over the years I've found this method of travelling mostly produces a wonderful feeling of adventure; when looking at the big picture I know where I am and where I'm going. In the little picture, however, I'm completely lost, which I love.

You may have noticed the word 'mostly'. Sometimes my lackadaisical method of travel, combined with the lack of brains in my Garmin, produces, shall we say, unintended side effects. These have been known to include (but are not limited to) shortcuts through people's gardens, dead ends, roads only for mountain goats, going round in circles, getting trapped in one-way systems and last but certainly not least, my favourite—having my fully loaded bike towed backwards up a steep and narrow path after coming to a closed gate late at night while being eaten alive by mosquitos and swearing profusely.

As I sat there in the comfortable surroundings, I smiled smugly as I thought about the grumpy bikers with their high-stress levels and their precise routes and fixed destinations. The smile disappeared when my brain conjured up the word 'Belgium'.

With my glass empty it was time to find a campsite. Time was still on my side, so I rode around the area looking for signs but to no avail. After exhausting the town and surrounding roads I decided to look a little further afield and took a turn in a westerly direction. Before long the scenery switched from town to idyllic countryside and the road opened up nicely. As I pottered along at a rather sedate 50mph, I noticed a strange noise. I eased up on the throttle, but it made no difference. Then it started getting louder. Not a second later I was passed by an Aprilia RSV-R racing bike. It must have been going 100mph minimum and made one hell of a noise as it flew past. I was full of envy as I watched it disappear into the distance, imagining the wonders of a fast and sporty bike on these roads. He was having some serious fun!

I know the Aprilia RSV-R as I had one for a year or so about five years ago. Its beautiful Italian lines were a perfect match for the violent acceleration, agile handling and intimidating exhaust note. It was a racer and designed for the track and as such, comfort was not high on the designer's list of priorities. That didn't matter if you were just popping down the road for a short spin but anything more than about thirty miles and various parts of one's body would start to shut down.

I caught up with the Aprilia a few miles down the road in some light traffic and it looked like the poor man was suffering. He was continuously moving around in his seat, straightening his legs one at a time and swerving all over the road. On his back he wore a large rucksack and behind him was what looked like a tent and an oversized duffle bag.

'Bloody hell, the man's camping!' I said in disbelief. 'On an RSV!'

The more I watched, the more intrigued I became. After a few more miles we came up against a red traffic light. He stopped, failed to get his foot down and the bike just fell over. As I clambered off my bike to help, two of his riding companions passed me and jumped in. One took the bike and the other helped the poor rider, who struggled to walk. I don't know how far he'd ridden but even 100 miles on one of those deserved a medal.

With all my bike envy gone, I got back on mine. With its reasonably comfortable seat and upright riding position it was a million miles away from the Aprilia; something I was pleased about, bearing in mind I probably had another 5,000 miles to go. As I rode off down the road deep in thought about how horrid it must be covering serious miles on a racing bike, I spotted a familiar sign. On it was a picture of a tent. Within minutes I was at the reception of a campsite. I looked around, trying to work out if it was nice or not. There were far more tents than caravans and camper vans, and the people milling around all looked happy. I was sold. I paid eleven Euros for the night and was told to follow the lady to my pitch.

'It's complicated,' she said.

She was right. I followed her for about 50 yards along an upper path, then turned left into pitch sixteen, bounced over the divide, squeezed between a car and a tree and by this time I was completely lost and stopped trying to remember the route. It was surprising in both its length and its height. When we finally reached my pitch, she pointed to the reception building about 100 yards away and 50 yards below.

'Bloody hell,' I said. 'Nice view.'

'Yes,' she said with a smile, 'no sleepwalking.'

'No, no sleepwalking.'

I thanked her for her help. She walked to the edge and

looked down at reception, about-turned and went back the way we came. Probably a wise choice.

I removed my jacket and stood there for a while looking at the view. It was high but not overly pretty. The grass, on the other hand, was soft and even and would make a wonderful base for my tent. After half a bottle of lukewarm Diet Coke, I set up camp. About 20 minutes later the tent was up, camping mattress inflated, sleeping bag laid out, leathers made into a pillow and everything organised in an anal fashion. I poured a large coffee and grabbed my iPad, camera and the exercise book I'd be scribbling notes in. It was time to write my blog. The following hour came and went, then another and slowly but surely the day's blog came to life. Once happy I activated my mobile hotspot, connected my iPad and uploaded it all to Facebook and my website.

'Aaah, my job is done,' I said, attempting to stand.

Despite pains in my right knee, hips and back, I managed—with the help of a reasonable amount of grunting—to get to my feet. I stood for a while, thinking about how I didn't have to make such stupid noises when I went camping as a younger man. My body was giving me jip from sitting with my legs crossed for two hours while writing. I've tried sitting in various positions but nothing else seems to work. I made a mental note to keep my eyes open for a decent camping chair that can fit on a bike, knowing that by the time tomorrow came around, I'd have forgotten it completely.

Leaning back against the bike I sat on the grass with my legs stretched out in front of me and watched the world go by as the sun disappeared and the night took hold. I thought about making a plan for the next day but decided against it. After all, plans are for amateurs.

Mileage for the day was 261 miles, bringing the total for the trip so far to 719 miles.

DAY THREE

You Furka!

AFTER WHAT can only be described as an exemplary night's sleep I woke to the wonderful sound of near silence. I unzipped the tent and poked my head out into the open and was presented with a biker's paradise. The sun was yet to achieve the necessary height to turn the sky from a mysterious deep blue void into the pale blue of its daytime counterpart. The day was indeed young, and the world was my oyster.

'Morning bike,' I said, exiting the tent. 'You ready for the D76?'

I checked my watch to find it wasn't yet 6am but I'd had enough sleep and was keen to get my wheels rolling. I poured a coffee as I studied the map, a rough route slowly forming in my mind. First, the bike and I would make our way back to Saint-Jean-en-Royans about 15 miles away. From there we'd enjoy the wonders of the

45

D76, a road I'd seen on the internet and in magazines many times. The end of the D76 is marked by a town called Col de Rousset. Once there I'd set my GPS for Chamonix and we'd meander our way to Switzerland in a leisurely manner, enjoying the winding mountain roads as we went. Lovely!

I glanced towards the reception building and thought how simple it would be to get there if I took the quick way down. I pushed the thought from my head and concentrated on packing up my stuff. Job done, I walked to the edge of the slope. It looked okay except for that it was incredibly steep. I noticed that the gap between the bottom of the slope and reception was of a reasonable size which should allow me enough time to slow down and stop. I was trying hard to persuade myself that it was a good idea, but that slope...

I looked over my shoulder at the other way down. I didn't know the exact route, but it was plain to see I'd have to ride through four or five occupied pitches and doing so before 7am didn't seem like a nice thing to do. I'd either have to wait or go down the quick way. I decided to clamber down the slope and take a look from the bottom.

I slipped and stumbled most of the way down but recovered by the time I reached the bottom.

'Bloody hell,' I mumbled, as I looked up at the slope from the other end.

I took a deep breath and let it out in a big sigh, knowing I had already made my decision. As I struggled to get back up, my mind insisted on imagining the sound my bike would make if it cartwheeled its way down. Luckily, I didn't have any confidence to lose at this point.

I checked I'd not forgotten anything, manhandled the bike so it was pointing the right way and climbed aboard. Sometimes using one's brain is the wrong thing to do so I switched mine off. I started her up, tapped the gear lever and stood up on the pegs. The elevated view I had from standing on the pegs made it look even worse.

'Christ almighty!' I exclaimed as I rode over the edge.

I sped down the slope like my arse was on fire. Even though it looked quite smooth from a distance, the slope proved to be anything but, bouncing me around to the point where I couldn't grab the brakes. By the time I'd reached the bottom I'd picked up quite a pace and stopping before smashing through the reception wall seemed most unlikely. I slammed on my anchors and just about managed to stop as a lady came running towards me.

'I've never seen that before!' she said, looking most shocked.

It's always good to have a witty one-liner ready for situations such as these.

'Bye.'

That and a smile was all I could manage, so full of shock and adrenaline was I. As I rode off, I looked in my mirror. The lady was standing there with both hands on her face, looking up at the slope. I got a feeling that my dodgy descent was going to be her dinner table story for quite some time.

The ride to Saint-Jeans-en-Royans was beautiful. The hazy air told me it was going to be another hot day. I arrived just before 7am and pulled over to examine the map. There wasn't really much to it, get on the D76 and stay on it until the village of Col de Rousset. It was no more than about twenty-five miles and shouldn't take long.

The whole reason I decided to head this far south was because of that next twenty-five miles. I left Saint-Jean-en-Royans with high expectations and hoped it wasn't going to disappoint. As I set off, I noticed I was completely alone; I had the road entirely to myself. It twisted, doubled back and twisted some more while climbing ever higher. The smell of pine and the cool air made it feel like a real alpine adventure.

After a few miles I reached the part where all the photographs are taken. It was indeed impressive but I'd bigged it up so much in my head it was almost inevitable I'd find it all a bit disappointing. I tried to appreciate it for what it was but there was no getting around the fact that it wasn't what I was expecting. From the photographs, it looked like there was a huge drop to the left of the road but in reality, it wasn't actually that high. The road itself though was wonderfully small and wiggly and the views were beautiful.

After about 15 minutes the road became less interesting, so I turned back in the opposite direction. Amazingly, I rode without seeing another single vehicle. Even though I found the actual road a bit disappointing, the experience of riding a mountain road early in the morning with no other people around was one I would remember fondly.

When I reached the village of Col de Rousset, marking the end of the D76, I stopped, looked over the map and set Chamonix as my destination. The next step of my journey would take me to closer to the full-blown mountains of the Alps and I could feel the excitement as I rode ever closer, my mind full of imagined images and stories I'd read. Unfortunately, just as I was expecting the mountains to appear on the horizon I found myself in the most horrific traffic jam.

'Well this wasn't a part of the plan, old girl,' I said, trying to keep my emotions in check.

I checked my GPS and found it had taken me into the arrhythmically beating heart of Grenoble. It was complete and utter gridlock, yet strangely calm. Nothing moved for the best part of an hour. The heat pressed down and cars pumped out their fumes but not a single horn was heard. No vehicles tried to turn around or find a better route and there were no shouts of frustration. A patient bunch were these Grenobleians! Is that a word?

Even though I was overheating, dressed in my Klingon outfit as I was, I felt the right thing to do was to be patient. To be honest, there wasn't a great amount that could be done. The bike was big, and the gaps were small. So, I waited.

And I waited.

And I waited.

Eventually, the traffic moved, and I saw what the problem was. Up ahead was a very large hole, some roadworks and a set of four-way traffic lights. A big lorry had decided it was not going to play ball and tried to take a shortcut across some grass. Unfortunately, it got to the worst possible point and promptly sunk. Slowly but surely, we were directed around the clot and before I knew it, we were on the other side. However, my elation was cut short after just a few seconds when I spotted the next traffic jam.

'Oh, I don't believe it!' I said, my head collapsing onto my tank bag.

I glanced around to see if there was anywhere to work my motorcycle magic but there were no suitable options.

'Bollocks to this. It's time for a coffee.'

I bounced my motorbike up onto the path and stopped its hot engine. After being cooked from the heat of the sun and by the hot air being blown onto my legs from the radiator fan, getting off and removing my jacket was a real pleasure. As the sweat evaporated from my stinky body I opened my left pannier and removed my Thermos flask. I frowned when I felt the lack of weight and swore when I discovered it was completely empty. I looked up the road at the never-ending traffic jam and noticed a large M sign. It was McDonald's—I was saved!

I tied my jacket to the back of the bike, put my helmet on and slowly rode along the path to the McDonald's, stopping a few times to let concerned pedestrians pass safely. When I reached the entrance, I was presented with a set of weird barriers and high curbs which stopped me in my tracks. I thought about what to do for about a thousandth of a second, then bounced over the lot of them and into the car park. It wasn't the most elegant of arrivals, but it was, indeed, an arrival.

The last time I'd attempted to buy coffee at McDonald's I'd tried speaking French and completely buggered it up, so this time instead of speaking French badly, I'd speak in perfect English and be proud. When I reached the front of the queue, I said: 'Good morning gentlemen. I'd like six large cups of your finest coffee please, strong and black if you don't mind.'

I'm not sure what I expected but I certainly didn't expect the response I got.

'That's no problem, sir, we'll have them ready for you in two shakes of a lamb's tail.'

It turned out that the chap who was serving me was English. He had studied politics at Birmingham and was having a few months out before getting a job. What a stroke of luck. I paid the man a small fortune, filled my Thermos and went back to my motorbike. As I stood baking in the car park but enjoying my coffee, I observed the slow-moving traffic.

'Riding through that shit's not going to be fun.'

I paused for a bit as I experienced one of those 'I'm bloody here and doing it' moments.

'I suppose it's that shit that we're here for. Grenoble, here we come!'

My little bit of shouting left me with renewed excitement but after just 50ft, the traffic stopped once more and the feeling instantly disappeared. The next 20 minutes weren't fun. Stop-start traffic, hot day, hot bike, the GPS having a nervous breakdown. It turned out that even Grenobleians have a limit to their patience. The traffic eventually thinned out and sped up, the bike cooled down and the GPS chilled out a bit.

I was trying to contort my upper body into a funnel to scoop some of the fast-moving air into my jacket when I spotted a sign for Le Champ. That was it, I just had to stop. A simple selfie would not suffice as I wanted the bike, the sign and me in the photo, so I removed my tripod and camera from the pannier and set up. For some reason I found myself rushing. My heart was beating away ten to the dozen and I refused to even glance at the passing cars. What the bloody hell was going on?

'This is bollocks,' I said, forcing myself to relax. 'Come on Mr Georgiou, why are you so bloody uptight?'

I thought about the question for a few minutes as I searched for the quick-release gizmo for the tripod. I felt like a naughty boy and that the right thing to do was to give up on the photograph and be on my way. Instead, I decided to simply lean against the bike and stop. I hate feeling scared and tend to rebel against it. I immerse myself in it and more often than not, the fear proves not to be that scary after all. So, there I was doing my level best to goad this fear by leaning against my bike and looking into the eyes of each and every driver who passed when a truck sounded his air horn in two long blasts. He gave me a thumbs-up and a cheesy grin. Inside of ten seconds, my heart was back to normal and the feelings of fear were relegated to my mental bin.

'Well that was useful wasn't it? Not!'

I found the gizmo for my tripod and finished setting it all up without any further rubbish from my irrational emotions.

Now, my camera seems to have the most complicated self-timer in the entire history of self-timers. You can't just, say, wait ten seconds and take a photo, you have to program the thing! I did the programming, told it to take ten photographs in case I blinked at the critical time and hit the go button. I darted in front of the camera and struck my best pose. Nothing happened. I waited a while longer but still, nothing happened. After standing there like a prize idiot for what must have been 30 seconds, I gave up and walked back towards the camera. It was at this point that the camera decided to take the first photograph.

'Bloody hell,' I said, making my way to the bike for the second shot.

When I got back in position, I raised my arms in the air, smiled and waited for the camera to soot. After 20 seconds with my arms in the air, my smile had turned into a frustrated grimace. I did my best to keep my eyes on the camera but the shouts and hoots that came from amused drivers were hard to ignore so I took a bow. It was at this point the camera took the second photograph. I lowered my arms and looked at the bike.

'Okay, it seems we have about 40 seconds between each photograph,' I said.

Another car bibbed so I waved at the driver. The next one stuck his head out of the window and shouted 'Adriaaaaan!' and held up a shaking fist. I recognised this immediately as the famous scene from the Rocky film and did some jogging on the spot to show my appreciation. It was then that the camera decided to take the third photograph.

'Okay Rich, you've had your fun,' I said, still smiling at the Rocky reference. 'Let's just get a photo, shall we?'

I raised my arms and smiled, doing my level best to look like a gnarly biker with a friendly slant. My patience was rewarded as the camera took its fourth photograph. To my absolute horror, when I checked the images, they were all completely out of focus. Like an idiot, I'd left the camera on manual focus.

'<Unprintable string of graphic expletives!>'

After a deep sigh, I switched the camera to autofocus and set it up again. I made my way back to the bike, posed like some teenage selfie queen and waited. Not even the wolf-whistling trucker could budge me from position until the photograph was taken. Click. I checked the photo.

'That'll do.'

The rest of the ride was beautiful with huge mountains, alpine views and superb roads. As I neared Chamonix, I looked for Mont Blanc but with so many huge mountains in the vicinity, it was hard to tell which one it was. Being that it's only 15,774ft high and the highest mountain in the Alps and, indeed, in Europe, I felt a little sheepish about asking people where it was but ask I did. Unfortunately, the three people I asked resulted in three different answers. At this point, I switched from being excited about seeing Mont Blanc to being excited about having *probably* seen Mont Blanc.

Having left so early, time was on my side, so I decided to ride around Chamonix for a bit, then to head off into Switzerland. Like everywhere in the Alps, Chamonix was incredibly scenic. It was coloured a rich green with huge mountains, outstanding views and had lots of little highly manicured streets containing wooden villas and chalets and rolling hills.

From Chamonix I took the D1506 through Argentiere and Vallorcine. I then hopped over the border which wasn't there into Switzerland. The road that goes from the border to the first town, which is called Martigny, is simply breath-taking and as windy as roads get. As an entry into Switzerland it was perfect.

From Martigny, I used a combination of the 9 and smaller roads to make my way through Saxon, Sion and Visp. As I meandered around the mountain roads, I spotted a sign to a place called Furka. Being a man with a dubious sense of humour (!) I found it worryingly funny saying 'You Furka!' every time I saw it on a sign. I switched to the 19 at Brig and continued through Obergoms towards

Andermatt. I stumbled upon a campsite by accident after 278 wonderfully twisty and breath-taking miles.

I'd forgotten about arming myself with Swiss Francs so was relieved when the chap at reception asked if I wanted to pay in Francs or Euros. I pulled out a concoction of cash, petrol and food receipts, a half-eaten Snickers bar and a slightly snotty handkerchief and handed over 12 Euros. In return, I was given a half franc coin.

'For the showers,' I was told.

My place for the night was disappointingly flat but it was quiet, had reasonable views and a nice open feel. I did a circuit, then picked my spot next to an immaculate BMW R1200GS Adventure. On the other side was a big Yamaha Tourer. I managed to set up camp inside of about ten minutes. Just as I was about to attempt conversation with my rather serious looking neighbour, I caught a whiff of my most unpleasant odour.

'Christ almighty.'

The last time I'd smelt something like that the poor sod was sleeping on a layer of cardboard. I found the franc, grabbed a fresh pair of pants and then revelled in the most wonderful of showers. It was the perfect temperature and power, and the liquid soap stuff I had with me smelt glorious. It washed away my stink perfectly. Just as I reached the point of peak lather there was a little click, and the water stopped. I stood there, covered with a not insubstantial amount of soap and bubbles, in complete darkness and wondered what to do next. Without a great deal of options, I did my best to wrap my tiny hand towel around my dignity and make my way to reception for another franc.

It took quite some time to cross the 100 yards or so, holding onto my towel for dear life. Luckily, I was so busy trying to get the liquid soap out of my eyes that I didn't notice my audience. Upon reaching reception the chap kindly handed me another franc, smiled and wished me the best of luck returning to the shower unscathed. I made it back—past openly laughing children, gossiping ladies and grinning teenagers—and took the other half of my shower. Sud-free and smelling fresh, I made my way back to the bike. I looked over at my neighbour, but he seemed very busy tinkering with things. I decided not to share my story. Instead, I poured a coffee and got down to some serious blog writing.

My style of writing is what I call 'delete and repeat'. I put something down, read it and then decide whether to keep, delete or rewrite it. Most of the time I rewrite a few times before I'm happy. As such, writing my evening blog takes a while. After an hour of sitting on the ground cross-legged, I needed a break. I attempted to stand but my feet had gone numb and my hips were killing me. I gradually got up and enjoyed the warm feeling of my feet coming back to life. The pleasure didn't last long though, as soon enough they were alive with a serious bout of pins and needles.

After a few minutes of oohing and aahing, I settled down and continued writing. A couple of hours later it was uploaded and that, as they say, was that. Before I clambered into my sleeping bag, I checked my blog. One of my mates had sent a message.

'You must ride the Furka Pass, you Furka!'

I checked it out on the internet, and it turned out that he was right.

Mileage for the day was 278 miles, bringing the total for the trip so far to 997 miles.

DAY FOUR

Popping and Farting

WOKE AT 5.40am to the noise of my neighbour tinkering with his BMW. The zip on my tent door was broken so I had a clear view of the proceedings, and my frustration at being woken so early was replaced by fascination.

He attentively checked his oil level and tyre pressure. The front must have been microscopically low because he attached a flashy electric pump and turned it on for literally two seconds. He checked the pressure again and smiled, folded up the instruction booklet and packed it back into its box. He then took out an expandable pole and stuck it into the ground about 10ft in front of his bike. I was intrigued. He switched his bike on and checked the headlight was hitting the right mark on the pole. Crikey. Now that is what you call attention to detail!

Taking his tent down was equally as detailed. Each of

the guy ropes was loosened, unfastened and then folded before carefully packing them into their own little baggies. Before taking the tent down, he wiped it over with a cloth, then took the cloth to the sinks and washed it. He hung the cloth on a mini washing line that extended from his panniers to his handlebar. When the washing line sagged a little, he adjusted the tension. This went on and on and on. Camping on a motorbike is not easy at the best of times but with a serious dose of OCD, it must be almost impossible. Still, he seemed to be enjoying himself.

With everything packed up, he sat on his bike. Dressed in the full complement of BMW gear, he looked like a living, breathing BMW advert. I thought he was just about to ride away but no, there were lots more checks and tests to perform. He checked his brake light, front and rear indicators and other things I think only BMW people know about. After about ten minutes of tests and checks, the chap in the tent on his other side stuck his head out of the door and shouted at him. I don't know exactly what was said but I think it was the Swiss version of 'will you just fuck off!' and with that, he rode away.

Observing Mr BMW's military precision made my effort seem a little sloppy. I took everything out of my tent and stuffed it all into my panniers, took the tent down and stuffed it into its bag, tied it all to the bike and buggered off. The bike is a Honda so there is no need to check the oil, tyre pressures or headlight alignment. <Grin>. I did check the map though. It turned out there were a number of passes in the area, so I wrote down some village names and rode to them one by one.

My morning was spent riding around Switzerland experiencing the delights of the Furka Pass, the Grimsel Pass and the Susten Pass. Much of the riding was spent at altitude and with the bike being of a 2006 vintage, it had carburettors. These antiquated little beauties are wonderful at the lower levels but the moment one passes the dizzy heights of about 3,500ft they develop a slight stammer. I noticed a distinct lack of power as I passed 4,500ft. By 5,500ft the lack of power had been joined by a kind of misfire. At 7,500ft I experienced what can only be described as a seismic backfire. This was immediately followed by a seismic piece of hearty flatulence.

As I climbed ever higher my speed reduced until I struggled to get out of second gear. At one point, with the throttle about 50 per cent open, I could only manage around 20mph. Interestingly, if I opened the throttle fully there was a pause where it felt like it was going to die completely, then after a number of pops and farts, it would burst into life and fire me at the next hairpin. Sometimes I used full throttle but with the roads being so bendy, I had to be careful. Struggle as the bike did, it refused to let me down and continued like a true workhorse. I could see my fouled plugs in my mind but there was little I could do about it, so I pushed on and hoped against hope that the problem would miraculously go away all on its own.

Going up was exciting in a 'what's next' kind of way and going down was exciting in a fun kind of way. The bike didn't have to push against gravity any longer and became more powerful the more we descended. This gave it a sporty feel which brought out the racy side of me. I whizzed around the bends at God only knows what speeds. Each bend I successfully negotiated increased my confidence and just as I thought I'd achieved the pinnacle of riding prowess, I was rudely overtaken by a small, red and decidedly knackered looking, postal van. It took the bends like it was being driven by the Stig himself. I tried to keep up for a while, but it was blatantly obvious that I was completely out-classed.

Feeling a little sheepish I slowed back down and let my riding style return to 'ageing granny' where it belonged. When I had descended to something like sea level, I decided to stop for a coffee but found my flask almost empty. I also needed fuel, so stopped at the nearest petrol station and filled up. Leaving the bike, even if it's just for a minute or two, is a real ordeal. I go through the motions of removing my GPS and tank bag and locking everything that's left. Then I don't let the bike out of my sight for more than a few minutes. All this means that stopping anywhere is a real pain in the backside so, being an inherently lazy person, I decided to relax a bit and start trusting people a little more.

With this in mind, I pulled into the station and stopped next to the pump. I filled up and walked into the shop to pay. It was so nice not lugging my helmet, gloves and

GPS around with me and not feeling the need to look at the bike every ten seconds. I wandered around the shop feeling I'd really turned a corner as far as trust was concerned. I used their machine to make a few large black coffees for the flask, found a nice-looking chicken sandwich and a jar of instant coffee, then joined the queue to pay. As I stood there feeling surprisingly relaxed about the whole thing, I decided this was a far better way to travel. I didn't look at the bike again until I arrived at the front of the queue.

'Oh, er, numéro de la pompe...'

I glanced at the bike to find a van stopped next to it. Leaning out of the window was a thieving bastard trying his hardest to remove GPS from my handlebar.

'Oi!' I shouted, hurriedly putting my coffees on the counter.

I continued with a bit of verbal abuse as I ran out of the shop and towards the van. Most wisely, the thieving bastard had seen me coming and decided to skedaddle before getting his face smashed in. The van sped out of the station's forecourt just in time. I shouted some more obscenities as the van sped away, then promptly removed the GPS from the handlebar and tucked it safely into my pocket. Before making my way back to the shop, I grabbed my crash helmet and gloves and locked my tank bag and panniers.

'Perhaps I won't trust people quite yet,' I muttered.

The checkout lady asked if I wanted her to call the

police. I just about managed to stop myself from telling her not to worry as I was going to hunt him down and kill him. Instead I thanked her for her concern but didn't want to be hanging around for ages, so told her not to worry as nothing was actually stolen. She patted my shoulder and said she was sorry. Sweet.

As I rode out of the forecourt, I ran the previous ten minutes through my mind. Luckily the thieving scumbag struggled to rub two brain cells together and, as such, failed to work out that if he had pressed the release button, the GPS would have simply fallen into his hands. Perhaps paranoid is the right trust level to have when touring on one's motorbike. With a bitter taste in my mouth, I rode into Selva. It was beautiful but my mood remained dark. I stopped and took some photographs and rode down some spectacular side roads, but I was angry.

'The bloody audacity! Who gives him the right to take my stuff?'

Although the bike didn't respond, I was quite sure it understood. I imagined the pleasure of catching him and giving him a good punch on the nose. I could feel my anger getting stronger and stronger. This was not good. I needed to get out of this cycle. I looked around at my surroundings.

'Yeah, yeah, it's beautiful. So what?'

And that's when I spotted a line of ladies up ahead.

As I rode closer, I got my first clear view. The line was comprised of about fifty young ladies in single file. They were all dressed in tight Lycra shorts, small tops and not a great deal else. On their feet were roller skates and they pushed themselves up the slight incline using two ski poles, one in each hand.

'Mary mother of God!' I laughed into my helmet.

My bad mood instantly disappeared and was replaced with a bemused 'thank God I'm alive' kind of mood as I smiled from ear to ear. I slowed down and sat a little way behind the lady at the back, working out what to do. Luckily the road was very twisty, so I had to overtake each lady one at a time, making sure the road was completely clear before each one. Concentrating was quite difficult as the ladies insisted on poking their bottoms out and wiggling them around quite a lot but concentrate I did. Unfortunately, it only took a few minutes to zip past the skiers but on the bright side, the memory of them will last much longer.

Using a dodgy combination of GPS, map, compass, 'the Force' and road signs I continued on the 19 through Laax, Flims and Trin then turned onto the 3 at a place called Chur. I stayed on the 3 for a while but the road wiggled around and before I knew it, I was lost. When I found myself again, I was in the town of Surava. Using the compass to guide me, I made my way through Schmitten and Wiesen. Just before reaching Davos the bike began messing around. The engine still worked but was lumpy as hell. I pulled over and poured a coffee. Then I started up the engine but the moment I released the throttle, it immediately stalled.

I'm not a natural mechanic and my methods normally involve things like swearing, kicking and wiggling things until it jumps into life, but before I did any of that I thought it would be a good idea to see if anything obviously wrong stood out.

I took off my jacket, hung it on the handlebar and examined the side of the engine. The first thing I saw was a small rubber pipe. One end was connected to the petrol tank but the other end wasn't attached to anything. I then noticed a small connector on the front of the rear cylinder. I popped the pipe onto the connector and started up. It ran perfectly. I stood back and bowed, all proud and all.

'It was nothing, no, really, no need to thank me.'

The warm glow I felt from the combination of caffeine and being a mechanical genius felt good. When I finished my coffee I took another look at the rubber pipe and found that the end was stretched and out of shape. No wonder it fell off. With some length to play with, I cut the end off and fixed it firmly back in place. A job well done. Perhaps it was just in my mind but as I rode into Davos the bike seemed to be smoother than ever; surprising considering the town sits at around 5,000ft.

Given that Davos plays host to the World Economic Forum I thought I'd ride around and take a look. I noticed the whole place was like some kind of unlived in immaculate show home. Every green area was manicured to within an inch of its life, every building looked clean and freshly painted, and even the birds seemed to sing in unison. It was so bloody perfect that I almost sick-burped in my helmet. I thought riding around on my scruffy bike in my stinky leathers would make people uncomfortable but quite the opposite was true. Everyone seemed to smile at me, but with perfectly aligned paper-white teeth, I felt even more out of place. Just when I thought I was going to drown in niceness, my bike came to the rescue with an incredibly loud backfire. One of the previously smiling ladies cowered and covered her head with a folder. The other one ran for cover.

Sniggering, I decided it was probably a good time to leave but when I opened up the throttle there were a few jerks and then the bike stopped altogether.

'No!' I exclaimed. 'Anywhere but here, please no!'

I pulled in the clutch and pressed the starter. The engine turned over but refused to catch, then BANG! After another glorious backfire, it started, and I gently rode out of Davos towards the delights of Austria.

I'm far from being an expert at such things but I think the combination of the bike having a carburettor, being at high altitude and the fact I was riding around town at 5mph pretty much on tick over was all a little too much for the fuelling. As I left Davos, I opened up the throttle and the bike stuttered around for a bit but then seemed to settle down. I made a mental note to check the internet for solutions to such problems once I'd set up camp for the night.

From Davos I took the 28 to the town of Susch where I then joined the 27. This took me through Lavin,

Scoul, Ramosch and finally Martina which is at the border. The border is actually a river, so it was over the river and into Austria. There were no signs or indications that I'd left or entered another country, which I found a little sad. I like to think I'm riding through separate countries with their own traditions and identities. Perhaps I'm just an old fart.

I followed the 185 to Nauders, turned onto the 180 and made my way north through Vinadi, Pfunds, Lafairs, Tösens, Fließ and Rifenal. I was getting tired and looking forward to setting up camp. The GPS found a campsite just outside of Innsbruck. Perfect. I followed the magenta line on the screen which took me through some nice little villages and concluded with me sitting right outside the rather nice-looking site.

After the ten minutes it took to set up, I sat on the ground, poured a coffee and ate my chicken sandwich. It took just under two hours to complete my blog and another ten to upload it. I congratulated myself with another coffee and sat for a while watching dark storm clouds approach, flashing alive with lightning. It didn't take long for the wind to whip up and then came the rain. It was time for bed.

Mileage for the day was 265 miles, bringing the total for the trip so far to 1,262 miles.

DAY FIVE

Tired and Grumpy

I LOVE A good thunderstorm as much as the next person but the one that woke me, after I'd been asleep for what felt like less than ten minutes, was angry. I poked my head outside the tent and witnessed a real spectacle of nature. The sky was alive with electricity and the resulting thunder exuded power which left me in no doubt of its deadly ability. I sat, fascinated, and watched it for a further hour before my eyes started to close.

At about 5am the trains started. When I arrived in the area, camping next to Innsbruck's airport sounded a little exotic and, as such, a good idea but at five in the morning I wasn't so sure. An hour later the planes started, and I got up. The overnight storm had left behind a beautiful morning. A layer of mist hung over the ground but the air above it was crystal clear. This and the warm light from the low sun gave it a beautiful yet eerie feel. I tried

69

to appreciate the fantastic mountain views but was so tired they just weren't sinking in. I poured a coffee and tried to conjure up some positive thoughts.

When I'd finished my drink, I inserted my earplugs, climbed back into my sleeping bag, closed my eyes and lay there, trying to sleep, for the next hour. The longer it went on the more frustrated I became and by the time I gave up I was consumed by grumpiness. Today was going to be a challenge.

'Bollocks, I'm getting up.'

Now, when I'm in a bad mood I tend to wallow in the negative and ignore the good. As such, the fact I was on a trip of a lifetime, on my motorcycle, surrounded by incredible views on a day with perfect weather was completely ignored. When I spotted the bike's wet seat, I exhaled a deep, miserable sigh.

'Great!' I said, raising my hands in the air. 'Now I've got to ride the whole day with a wet arse.'

I stomped back to the tent like a reprimanded eight-year-old, grabbed my T-shirt and used it as a cloth. I could feel the anger building and knew I had to put a stop to it before it started to bugger things up. I poured what was left of the coffee, sat on my sleeping bag and read the replies to last night's blog. To my surprise, one of my friends had posted a suggestion about how to help my bike with its severe altitude sickness. His advice was to use the best petrol I could find.

My mood improved and life wasn't that bad after

all. I spread out the map. As a part of preparing for the trip, I'd circled various places of interest but unfortunately hadn't said why. I hoped the reasons would become apparent when I arrived at them. I created a rough route that joined up the places I'd circled, entered it into the GPS, double-checked it and left.

From Innsbruck I took the 171 to Wattens, Pill and Buch, I then turned onto the 169 and headed south towards my first circled place of the day, Zell am Ziller. It was the kind of riding people like me go on trips like this for. The roads were superb, the weather was perfect, and the views were to die for. I had complete freedom to go wherever I wanted for a whole month. Life should have been like visiting Nirvana, however, I found myself riding along wondering what on Earth I was doing.

I followed the GPS's instruction to the letter and ended up in a decidedly dodgy-looking car park round the back of an abandoned station. The looks I received from the occupants of the three cars parked there told me I was not welcome. I rode around and back out again.

'What a lovely car park,' I said sarcastically. 'Just imagine if I'd have come all the way to Austria and missed that wonderful car park. And...' I continued, 'I wouldn't have had the pleasure of seeing the dogging locals.'

I shook my head and smiled into my helmet as I rode back to the 171.

The next circle on the map was Maria Alm. I rode through Brixlegg, Kundl and Wörgl, switched onto the

178, then the 164 to ride through Sankt Johann. Twenty minutes later I entered Maria Alm. It was pretty but no prettier than any of the other places I'd ridden through that morning.

'What am I doing?' I said, as I pulled over. 'What's the point of all this?'

It was a valid question and one I found very difficult to answer. I wasn't feeling the love. I got off, deep in thought. What the trip needed was some purpose, a destination, something to look forward to. I looked at the map and there it was: Salzburg. If it was good enough for the von Trapp family, it was good enough for me.

The roads along the way weren't any more beautiful than others I'd already seen, but now I had an exciting destination. I liked the sense of purpose.

'High on a hill was a lonely goatherd, layee odle layee odle lay ee oooh!'

When I arrived at Salzburg, I couldn't help myself and burst into song. Fortunately, for those around me, my crash helmet muffled most of the sound. At first, the traffic moved at a reasonable pace, but it didn't take long before it slowed down, then stopped altogether. The emotional high I'd felt on arrival in Salzburg pretty much disappeared as I got my first look at the scene up ahead.

No, no! It's Grenoble all over again,' I said, kicking myself.

After watching The Sound of Music with my moth-er-in-law, I had high expectations of Salzburg. My first impression of the place was one of complete chaos. The road leading in was being worked on and there was an incredibly slow traffic light system in place. On top of that, a few people decided not to wait, which buggered it all up completely. The workmen tried their best to sort it out by directing people all over the place but then a lorry decided to do it on his own and got stuck. It really was Grenoble all over again. After sitting there baking in the sun for half an hour, I plucked up courage and jumped off the road onto an adjacent field. Twenty minutes later I was stuck in stationary traffic in the heart of the city.

'This is madness,' I said to no one in particular.

When I saw a nice-looking restaurant, I pulled over and popped in. I asked if there was somewhere nearby park my bike, but the closest place was about 300 yards away. I tried another restaurant, but they had no parking either. As I was about to give up, I saw a restaurant with a big wide pavement outside. I rode the bike right up to the window and stopped. Excellent.

I secured everything as best I could but left it all on the bike. I was about to enter the restaurant when a police car pulled up and told me I couldn't park there. I asked him where I could park but the closest place was about a 20-minute walk away! I unstrapped my tank bag and gave it to the policeman. I removed my leather jacket and gave that to him too. Next was my crash helmet, which he placed under his arm. Then I removed my GPS and gave that to him.

'Could you walk 20 minutes with this lot?' I asked.

He understood my predicament, but it made no difference; I would still have to park in a designated place. I could feel my anger building and didn't want to end up spending the night in a cell so bit my tongue, thanked the officer for being so incredibly helpful, put all my stuff back onto the bike and rode back out into the traffic. As I sat there melting in the 34 degrees heat, I asked the GPS to get me the hell out of Salzburg.

The next hour was spent in combat with fellow road users as we all attempted to find the best way out. I never did see any of the beautiful buildings Salzburg is famous for, but I did, however, see a lot of traffic and a lot of restaurants I couldn't eat at. By the time I was clear, my mood had reached about four on the Richter scale. Knowing full well that it was down to my lack of sleep made it worse as it was all my fault.

'You've got no one to blame but yourself,' I said, forcing a smile.

It was time to stop. I pulled off down a side road and found a quiet spot to take a breather. My flask was empty, but I needed a caffeine fix so made an instant coffee using cold water. It didn't taste the best, but it did the job. As I drank, I tinkered with the GPS. Before embarking on this trip, I'd told it to record my track as I thought it would make for interesting viewing back home a month later. I looked at the route travelled so far, expecting to find a very wiggly magenta line zig-zagging its way from

Sussex to the exact spot in Austria I was currently occupying. To my horror, the wiggly line extended to just before Salzburg; it had recorded only the last few hours. Either I'd buggered something up or the GPS hated me, I think, probably both.

Having been let down by modern technology I decided to turn the clocks back and use something older and more reliable — the humble ballpoint pen. From this point forward, I would stop at every city, town and village and write down names on my pad. And I'd try really hard not to lose my pad.

The rest of the day took me through Puch, Oberalm, Kuchl, Golling, Tenneck, Mandling, Poham, Huittau, Espang, Liezen, Hall, Sankt Gallen and finally to a place called Landl, right in the middle of Austria. The ride was as scenic as ever, but I could feel my body going to sleep. At just before 7pm, I found a campsite. As I rode in, I could hear the wonderful sound of running water. The chap at reception told me there was a river at the bottom end. He also said there was a group of English kayakers staying. And he had pizza. That was it, decision made! I rode in and found my spot.

The site was positioned right on the river Enns, a southern tributary of the Danube, and was made up of three tiers. The first was the highest and comprised of reception, a kitchen and eating area. The next tier down was a long and reasonably narrow flat piece of land, ideal for camping. The bottom tier was a little wilder and right next to the river, which was quite a torrent and made a considerable amount of noise. I liked the idea of camping by the river, but the thought of some intelligent conversation won me over. I rode to the middle tier and set up camp not too close but not too far away from the English kayakers.

Assuming that smelling like an old tramp would hinder my chances of decent conversation I took a shower. Armpits smelling fresh, I made my way to the cafeteria and ordered a 'Bloody Hot Pizza' and a double whiskey. The pizza really was bloody hot, and to my absolute delight the double whiskey was basically a coke glass full of whiskey. With pizza and whiskey gone, I stumbled to my tent and did my level best to write my blog.

It was just gone ten when the English kayakers turned up. They were a group of around twenty youngsters between the ages of about 18 and 25, and they looked very friendly. I'm not great at initiating conversation but did my best.

'Hello,' I said to one of them walking past.

The chap looked over and smiled but didn't stop or say anything.

'Okay, Richard,' I muttered. 'That wasn't overly successful but that doesn't matter.'

I tried again.

'Hello, good day on the river?' I asked a girl.

She smiled but didn't say a word. Not wanting to appear too keen, I decided to continue writing and ignore them for a while. About an hour later I made my last attempt.

'Have you seen the size of their whiskeys here?' I said,

looking the chap in the eye to make it more difficult for him not to say anything. This is when I got my first response.

'Yes,' he said, and he continued on his way without stopping.

Wishing I'd camped by the river, I let out a deep sigh. I uploaded my blog and climbed into bed.

Mileage for the day was 260 miles, bringing the total for the trip so far to 1,522 miles.

DAY SIX

Carbonated Coffee

WELL, LAST night the hills were indeed alive with the sound of music. Unfortunately, most of it was by Dr Dre with some seriously kick-ass drum and bass. It didn't take long to find my earplugs and completely remove the outside world from my life. I slept like a baby until I was rudely woken by a very loud banging. I removed my plugs and poked my head outside the tent.

'What a bloody liberty,' I uttered under my breath, as I watched an elderly chap on the roof of a nearby building hammering nails into timber.

As tempting as it was to politely ask him if he would be so kind as to drop dead, I actually felt wide awake and in a good mood. I'd had such a solid night's sleep that I just didn't need anymore. I checked my watch; it was almost 6am.

I glanced at the talkative English kayakers, but their

tents were silent. How they could sleep through that banging was a complete mystery to me.

'Oh, the joys of being a youngster,' I said, in awe of their ability to sleep like the dead.

I watched the chap hammering as I finished a cup of cold but very strong coffee. Today was going to be a good day, I was in a good mood, and having had a large dose of sleep, nothing could change that. I packed up and checked the map before setting off. A few of the youngsters were up and I nodded in their direction. A few nodded too and waved me off, which was nice.

I rode to the end of my tier, up the dirt track to the top, then through the exit. From there I had to go back on myself to get on the main road. As I accelerated, I saw the group of talkative English kayakers, so I hooted my horn like an idiot and waved. To my surprise, they grinned and waved enthusiastically. Probably happy to get rid of an old fart.

It was good to be back on the road. Even though it was pretty much the same routine as the day before, it felt completely different. Simply being on the bike and riding through such a beautiful place was ample for my simple needs.

Everyone knows Switzerland and Austria are very well-kept and immaculately clean countries, but it wasn't until I got into the Austrian mountains that it really hit home. I was examining the road for rubbish, dumbfounded that I'd not seen any for miles and miles, when I noticed someone actually cleaning a road sign. I'd never seen this before. Another lady was washing the metal railings between her garden and the path. The mountains of Austria really are spotless. Half of me wanted to take the piss out of the place for its manicured pretence and for looking like a show home but the other half loved it.

I continued through Schönberg am Kamp, Plank am Kamp and Hagendorf to the border. These lower areas of Austria were very different to the mountains of earlier. Not only were they far less green, they were less manicured which gave them a more natural feel. There were weeds and the odd piece of rubbish in the road. Don't get me wrong though—in comparison to an English village it was still pretty much pristine.

Spending long periods of time riding through the idyllic countryside is all very well but it's never long before one's body starts playing up. First came the sore arse, promptly followed by an aching back. I tried doing all the things the long-distance biker does to keep the aches and pains at bay for a little longer. At one point I was happily riding along standing up on the pegs massaging my buttocks when an elderly couple in the car behind bibbed me. I could see their grinning faces in my mirror. I waved and they flashed me (with their headlights!), which made me smile. Unfortunately, all the fart-arsing around to get rid of my pains always seems to start my knees off. It was time for a break.

I pulled over just before Hausbrunn, about five miles shy of the border with Slovakia. I stood at the side of the road and had one of my special cold coffees and wondered what Slovakia would have in store. Even though my immediate surroundings weren't impeccably tended or mountainous, they still shouted Austria. I walked up and down, shook my legs and stretched my back.

A few minutes later I crossed the Morava River. There were no 'Welcome To Slovakia' or 'Good Riddance From Austria' signs — disappointing — but there were other indicators. The well-manicured look was replaced by a more wild, natural appearance which I preferred, and the beautiful roads of Austria were replaced by a patchwork of various surfaces and repairs. It felt more adventure and less holiday, which I liked. The rest of the afternoon was spent heading in a north-easterly direction towards the Carpathian mountains. Nothing changed much when I went from Switzerland to Austria but going from Austria to Slovakia saw a marked difference. It might sound like a negative by saying that Slovakia felt like it was behind by fifty years, but actually I mean that as a good thing. It didn't have smart road signs or complicated junctions, and the machinery in the fields looked more mechanical and less computerised. If I had to sum up the difference, I'd say it felt more honest. I think it would be fair to say, I was loving Slovakia.

After many miles and a long day in the seat, I felt more than ready to set up camp. Before long I found a site. When the chap at reception said the price was 35 Euros, I assumed I'd misunderstood and asked again. He repeated his answer. I felt like I was being bent over but as this was the first time camping in Slovakia, I wasn't sure. I tried really hard to just walk away but I felt my mouth open.

'Christ almighty! Does that include your daughter?'

Going by the look of shock-horror on the chap's face, I decided I would probably be best served elsewhere and promptly left. A bit further on I found another campsite. The lady smiled when I carefully asked the price.

'We are not 35 Euros,' she said, 'we are seven Euros.'

We laughed and I told her what I'd said to the chap up the road. She found that really funny and told the other receptionist, who gave me a high five. I was definitely liking Slovakia.

I chose a spot away from everyone, next to the woods, and set up. Before settling down to the task of writing my blog, I visited the onsite cafeteria and bar. I opened the door and was immediately confronted by a huge—and I do mean huge—bear skin hanging on the wall. From end to end it easily covered 8ft and gave me an insight into the power these incredible animals must have. The sheer mass of its head left me with a feeling of insignificance, and that feeling became even more pronounced when I spotted the size of its paws. They were about the same size as my torso.

'That's incredible!' I said.

'Yes,' said the waitress, handing me a menu. 'We used to have a big one, but it took up too much space.'

I told her I was going to be riding my motorbike

through the mountains in Slovakia and Romania. She looked back at me and smiled.

'You'll probably be fine,' she said, directing my attention to the menu.

I picked grilled chicken but unfortunately, they didn't have that, so I picked fried chicken with salad, but they didn't have that either. I was about to pick something else but was told they only had goulash. I had the goulash. And it was okay. As I walked back to my tent, I thought about my blog, but my mind kept returning to the bearskin and the phrase 'you'll probably be fine'.

When I'd researched the Carpathian mountains before leaving, it became apparent that being attacked by a bear was indeed a risk. Some of the horror stories I read really were very frightening and made me question whether I should be camping in the region at all. However, the kind of websites I trusted said that even just spotting a bear would be quite unlikely. That made me feel much better and I stopped worrying. Until spotting the giant bear skin in the cafeteria. It's a strange feeling not being at the top of the food chain.

I concentrated on my blog for an hour. Then I walked around for a bit trying to get some feeling back into my legs then attempted to make myself a coffee. Unfortunately, when I'd stopped at a supermarket earlier in the day, I'd bought four bottles of carbonated water by mistake. Cold instant coffee is quite horrid enough but adding fizzy water to the mix takes it to a completely new dimension. I had to eat my coffee with a spoon. I missed my stove.

With my caffeine needs satiated I finished writing and slept.

I had travelled through Pilfau, Gostling, Gaming, Muhling, Pulln, Erlauf, Ornding, Melk, Aggstein, Rossatz, Scholberg, Plank, Gars, Rosenberg, Horn, Grund, Hagendorf, Hausbrunn, Hohenau, Kuklov, Senica, Sobotist, Hrasne, Banov, Horne Vestenice, Benice, Martin, Sucany and Sutovo.

Mileage was 314 miles, bringing the total for the trip so far to 1,836 miles.

DAY SEVEN

FRIDAY, 23RD JUNE 2017

Hungary and the May Bugs

THE NOISE from an all-night storm pushed giant bears to the back of my mind and allowed for a solid night's sleep. I woke a few times throughout the night as I always do and listened to the rain on the tent walls. By the time I woke at about 6.30am I'd slept enough and was ready for adventure. However, with the storm still raging outside, it was probably best to wait for a while. I made another of my special fizzy coffees and read. It took a further two hours for the storm to pass.

Being in a new country is always exciting and Slovakia was no exception. After the polished and moneyed feel of Switzerland and Austria, I found myself revelling in Slovakia, though I couldn't quite work out why. Later in the day, it came to me: Slovakia felt less made and more grown. It wasn't made by man—it was a product of nature. Sometimes the natural element of rough and ready is far more beautiful than the highly manicured of prim and proper. I felt far more at home in Slovakia.

From leaving my campsite just outside of Sutovo, I joined the 18 and rode through Ivachnová to Lehota where I took a right onto the 72. The ride to Brezno was sublime, with hardly any traffic and stunning views of the Slovakian Carpathian mountains. I really felt I was in the adventure.

Turning up in Brezno was a bit of a shock. I'm sure the town has its nice parts but where I rode through didn't look good. As I accelerated away from a set of traffic lights a beaten-up old car containing a load of rough looking young men drove up alongside and attempted to wave me down. When I didn't stop, they held a bottle of brown liquid out of the window and waved me down more vigorously. I still didn't stop, which pissed them off completely. They pulled into my lane, trying to push me off the road and waved a bloody great knife out of the window. I opened up the throttle and sped off.

I decided not to stop for a while after that little episode and instead zipped along the 66 through village after village. In one of the towns I saw a huge billboard with a picture of Kylie on it. As I rode by, I raised my arms and blew her a giant kiss. A truck driver coming the other way noticed this and honked his air horn with two very loud blasts. As I looked over, he waved his hands out the window in a very funny breast squeezing gesture. It made me laugh and brightened up my day.

When I checked my odometer, I found I'd done 239 miles since filling up so began scanning the horizon for a petrol station. As the bike had been struggling with any kind of altitude my plan was to follow my mate Tim's advice and get the best fuel I could find. I passed the first garage I came to as it looked rather shoddy and I'd never heard of the brand. Next was a huge Shell station. Bingo!

I pulled in and examined my options. The picture for normal Unleaded 95 was of a businessman dressed in a grey suite answering a telephone. The picture for Super-Plus was of a huge, bald man dressed in a leopard-skin leotard and a wooden pole across his shoulders. Sat on either end of the pole were a couple of luscious ladies dressed in bikinis. I'm not sure I understood the message fully but decided Super-Plus was definitely the fuel for me. I immediately noticed the difference. At lower altitudes the bike felt far more responsive, even at just above tick over. At an altitude of 3,861ft (the highest that day), there was no sign whatsoever of any weakness. Fantastic! Thank you, Tim!

I turned onto the 67 just after Pusté Pole, then turned right onto the 587 just after Nižná Slaná, which took me south towards the Hungarian border. As I crossed over from Slovakia, I immediately felt the need to eat. Perhaps it was something in the name. I stopped at the first place I came to, parked the bike and made my way in. As I opened the door the noise stopped, and everyone turned and stared. Once again, a witty one-liner failed to surface and the first thing that came to me was a line from a film.

'Say! Any of you guys know how to Madison?' I said, looking round the room.

It wasn't the icebreaker I was after. Instead, everyone went back to their discussions and I took a seat. I looked for Hungarian goulash given I was in Hungary, but it was an egg-and-bacon kind of joint. I ended up with a chicken kebab and a salad.

I crossed the river Tisa at Árioktő, which was a nice experience. The little ferry zipped us from one side to the other and only cost a Euro.

I always thought of Hungary as a means of getting from Slovakia to Romania. I think the reason for that was a lack of mountains. Happily, I was surprised to find that after having ridden through a small piece of it, I was left with fond memories of luscious green scenery and the beautiful river Tisa. It was very flat though.

After covering about 250 miles, it was time to find a place for the night and I stumbled upon one literally ten seconds later. It was near a place called Hortobagy and the site itself was in the gardens of a small but posh hotel. It was very well tended but completely flat and not as rural as I'd become accustomed to. Ample signage directed me to a car park. I wandered into the hotel lobby.

'Er excuse me,' I said, feeling most out of place in my dirty and somewhat stinky leathers.

The chap behind the large and very grand reception

desk was impeccably dressed. Just looking at him made me want to turn and run.

'Aaah sir, here for the camping, are we?'

'Indeed I am. I wonder, would I be able to get a large bottle of still water and a strong, black coffee here?'

I asked cautiously, thinking he would want to get me out of the lobby as soon as possible.

'But of course, sir,' he replied, waving his hand towards a large leather sofa. 'If you'd like to take a seat, I'll be with you as soon as I can.'

I perched my bottom on the edge of the sofa, trying hard not to make a mess. I didn't have to wait long before the chap returned. I thanked him, paid for the pitch and made my way back to the bike. I soon found a nice spot, drank my wonderfully fresh coffee, set up camp and wrote. The blog complete and the sun edging below the horizon, I took out my newly purchased still water to find it was actually carbonated. After a big sigh, I made yet another of my special fizzy coffees and sat on a borrowed plastic chair to enjoy the moment. And that is when the fun started.

Out of the corner of my eye I spotted a bat, then another. Then I was hit on the head by what felt like a small acorn. I bent down to pick up the offending object when another one fell into my fizzy coffee like some kind of miniature asteroid. I tipped my coffee on the grass and discovered, to my amusement, that the little asteroids were, in fact, May bugs.

As the sun slowly disappeared and the sky grew darker, the battle between the bats and the bugs heightened into some kind of weird finale. The bats, being highly agile, flew rings around the bugs which, as far as I could tell, flew reasonably well in straight lines but hadn't quite mastered turning or landing. At one point, I was struck by a fit of the giggles when it all just went mad. I was being hit by bugs every few seconds and could hear the plucky little buggers bouncing off my tent and bike. I have no idea what May bugs are made of, but I have conclusive evidence that whatever it is makes fizzy coffee froth like nothing else I've ever seen, especially when entered at speed.

After half an hour or so, enough was enough. I climbed into my sleeping bag and drifted off to the land of nod with the sound of May bug Armageddon outside.

Mileage for the day was 249 miles, bringing the total for the trip so far to 2,085 miles.

DAY EIGHT

Vodka Flavoured Mineral Water

I WOKE AT about seven to a wonderful morning. It was a little cooler and completely still. I had Romania on my mind and was looking forward to seeing what it offered. The border was only about 60 miles away, so I was hoping to be in the Romanian Carpathian mountains by the afternoon.

I checked the map and plotted a rough route. My plan was to enter Romania at Ártánd and make my way northeast to the Carpathian Mountains. I'd then enjoy the riding as I followed the mountains in a large, backward C shape. Needless to say, my day didn't go according to plan.

When I reached Romania, I was happy to see a real-life border with guards, buildings and a queue. I joined the back and set about waiting patiently when I was hooted at, then told to ride to the front. Being English, I take a very dim view of queue jumping but who was I to argue with the locals? I pulled out and rode past the queue expecting to get some flak but there was none. When I reach the front, I was approached by a guard whom I'm sure was going to tell me to get to the back but nope, he pointed at a spot right at the front. I rode forward into the spot and listened attentively while he spoke in Romanian.

'English?' I said, hoping.

'Passport,' he replied.

He looked through it for about a minute and handed it back.

'Bike,' he said.

'Aaah, that'll be the logbook then.'

I opened the right pannier and removed the plastic pouch containing my paperwork. He took one look at the pouch and sighed.

'You can go,' he said and that was it.

I was in Romania. Even though it was just about the least stressful border I've ever crossed, it still made me feel a little bit manly which, when you're five foot four and not the brawniest of fellas, is quite a rare occurrence and something to be enjoyed. I felt a combination of exhilaration and anticipation. I'd done lots of research (looked at photos on the internet) on the Carpathian mountains and was keen to get among them. I stopped at the first opportunity and set a new destination into my GPS.

The first five minutes were spent riding through a

built-up area but once out into the open Romania didn't disappoint. The combination of green pastures, weird mounds of hay and a distinct lack of people made the riding a real pleasure. I indulged myself in the beautiful surroundings as I followed the magenta line on my GPS, hoping against hope it was taking me ever closer to the Carpathians. After half an hour, I found myself back at the border.

'Oh. That wasn't supposed to happen.'

I checked the GPS but what I saw didn't make any sense, so I dismounted and found my map. Being a map of Europe, Romania was tiny and had almost no detail, rendering the thing all but useless. I would have to rely on the map within the GPS.

I found a village about ten miles up the road called Roşiori and programmed it in. When it finished calculating the route, I gaped in disbelief. It wanted me to go back into Hungary, head in a north-easterly direction until I reached Ukraine, cross the border and continue east for about one hundred miles, then head south back into Romania, then switch back on myself and head west to my destination. All in all, a 443-mile trip! I looked over at the bike and shrugged. After wasting a further ten minutes sifting through loads of settings and getting more and more pissed off, I switched it off and reattached it to the bike.

'Useless bloody piece of vindictive shit. I'd get further using a map of my back passage.'

I found my compass, located north-east, found a hill to follow and checked my watch. Following a rough compass bearing was nice and easy except for once when I ended up in someone's driveway. As I got closer to the Carpathian mountains, I noticed families sitting outside their houses on benches covered with colourful rugs. At first it was just the odd few, but it wasn't long before almost every home had someone sitting outside. The children, more often than not, waved excitedly and grinned but the adults just stared as I rode past. Sometimes they allowed themselves a slight nod—but never anything more.

After about an hour of meandering in roughly the right direction, I came across a petrol station that served premium fuel. I filled up with the good stuff and ventured inside to pay.

Presented perfectly inside were a number of tables and chairs, a fully stocked display of cakes and a smiling lady ready to serve. On top of that, the air conditioning was incredibly effective, almost to the point of making it uncomfortable. I ordered two double espressos and a piece of carrot cake, then paused. I pointed to another cake that took my fancy,

'What is that?'

'We call it The Thing,' she said.

I added The Thing to my order and reached into my jacket pocket to get my wallet when the lady spoke.

'I have a hot muffin.'

The only sentence that entered my head was completely unacceptable and could well have landed me in a cell for the night, so I just stood there looking stupid. She held open the door to her microwave, and no, that's not a euphemism either. Inside was a nice, steaming hot chocolate muffin. I couldn't help letting out a laugh, but I don't think the lady understood quite what was going through my sordid little mind. I sat in the cool air enjoying my cake and coffee. The Thing turned out to be a glorious combination of chocolate, nuts, cream and ginger, and it slipped down a treat.

With my stomach and caffeine addiction fully satiated, I purchased a beautiful large-scale laminated map of Romania and a few bottles of still water from the lady with the hot muffin. I thanked her and smiled as I left.

After becoming acclimatised to the cool air inside, the heat outside came as a rude shock. I glanced at the map and was happy to see the way I'd come so far was pretty much on the money. When I approached the Carpathian mountains the condition of the roads quickly deteriorated. Large sections of the top surface had been removed, leaving a mixture of sand and stones to ride through. Most of it was no more than three or four inches deep so these were no problem for my trusty steed, but they hid deeper areas which I thought would be fun. They turned out to be not much fun at all. Luckily traffic lights meant that I could wobble my way over the whole road without the risk of crashing into oncoming vehicles.

As I continued to climb higher, the roadworks continued but traffic lights—or indeed any form of traffic management—completely disappeared. It was a fend-for-one's-self kind of set-up, which I quite liked. With other vehicles few and far between, I pretty much had the place to myself. The altitude had replaced the oppressive heat with cool air that was a pleasure to ride through and the gravelly sand went from being a little scary to seriously fun. I kept my speed down and enjoyed the power of second gear and going a little sideways.

I continued through the mountains and started thinking about a campsite for the night. My usual method was to look for possibilities in the late afternoon, but I'd not seen any signs since getting up into the Carpathians. I asked the GPS and it found Dimelza, 60 miles west.

The campsite was about five miles southeast of Cârlibaba and by the time I reached it, I was more than ready to get my backside off the seat. I was greeted by the friendly owner who showed me to a pitch. Before I could set up, he got his lawnmower out and mowed the pitch until it was perfect. With my tent up, I grabbed a few things and went to the bar for a drink, taking my pad to scribble notes about the day and try to write something that would later jog memories about places I'd been and experiences I'd, er, experienced.

Before I managed to get down anything substantial, I was joined by the owner. He was a super chap with a friendly demeanour and plenty of stories about travellers who'd stayed at his place. We chatted for a while when a lady approached the table and asked if I'd like to join her and her friends for some food later. Obviously, the answer was 'I'd be delighted, thank you'.

The bottle of beer the owner had kindly given me went to my head and I was about ready for food and more alcohol when the lady came back over.

'The food is ready,' she said, with a big smile.

The beer had removed my anti-social side and before I knew it, I was being introduced around. I said hello and a chap poured me a drink.

'Vodka flavoured mineral water,' he said, with a devious grin.

It turned out they were celebrating. One day each year, Romanians dress up in traditional costume and celebrate being Romanian. Luckily for me the celebrations included lots of barbecued meat and alcohol. I'd love to tell you all the intricate little details about the people, the food and the conversation but to be quite honest, after my first two water glasses of vodka, the memories are a little hazy. What I do recall is the incredible hospitality and generosity of the people.

With a stomach full of food and a head full of vodka, I stumbled back to my tent and stopped as I reached my bike.

'Get those tablets ready for the morning, old girl,' I said, already feeling a little worse for wear.

I collapsed into my sleeping bag and was immediately

engulfed by sleep. Mileage for the day was 278 miles, bringing the total for the trip so far to 2,363 miles.

DAY NINE

SUNDAY, 25TH JUNE 2017

A Scary Bit of Accidental Off-roading

N COMPLETE contrast to the details of the previous evening, my memory retained the morning's pain and discomfort in exquisite detail. My first thought on waking was that I'd gotten away with it. Then I made the mistake of moving slightly, and my head reminded me of the link between pleasure and pain. I remained still for a while, hoping the pain would go back to a dull throb but no such luck. I forced my body upright and searched around the tent for my Sigg water bottle. When I found it, my shaking hands struggled to remove the lid.

'Come on you bastard.'

I squeezed my hand around the lid and turned it with every muscle in my body. Finally, just before my temples exploded, I felt the thing budge. I tipped the whole litre of water down my throat and felt it absorb. After a minute or two, I swallowed down paracetamol and ibuprofen with another litre of water. I leant back on my sleeping bag and waited for the tablets to take effect.

Half an hour later I felt a little better and started wondering about breakfast. First though, I grabbed my toiletries and dragged my fragile body to the shower block. I stripped off. Before I could work out how to get the shower working, someone entered a nearby cubicle. I shall refrain from going into detail; suffice to say that my stomach was not in a strong enough state to cope with the hideous noises — not the mention the stench — that came from my neighbour. I grabbed my clothes and exited as quickly as I could before something terrible happened. With all thoughts of food completely vanished, I returned to my tent.

'Not the best appetiser I've ever experienced!'

Soon the toilet block ordeal was distant enough to start contemplating food once more. When I arrived at the breakfast table, I was greeted by the larger-than-life owner.

'Aaah, breakfast time!' he said, with a great big smile.

I agreed and told him I'd have whatever he was doing. A feast arrived. It was a selection of cold meats, a couple of fried eggs and a few unidentified things that looked edible. I did my level best, but my delicate stomach wasn't up to much so most of the food remained on the plate. I did, however, manage to get through a large pot of very strong coffee.

With my bike packed up and the bill, paid I said my goodbyes and departed for a nice relaxing Sunday morning ride through Romania. I rode slowly, enjoying the deserted mountains and the beautiful weather. For the first 20 minutes I didn't see a single soul. It was a surreal experience, like being in a zombie film. Then I spotted someone—an elderly chap dressed in an old worn suit, pushing a very tired-looking push bike. As I drew nearer, he stared at me with his mouth wide open. He let go of one of the handlebars and crossed himself in a Mary-Mother-of-God kind of way and continued staring as I rode by.

'That was weird,' I said, finding it a bit of a novelty.

A few miles down the road I spotted another person, this time a woman. She also had a push bike. As I approached, she stared like I was the Devil and crossed herself over and over again.

'Okay. Definitely weird,' I said, wondering what the bloody hell was going on.

This happened throughout the morning and left me feeling confused and a little concerned. The combination of the location, the weird crossing motion and the Sunday morning silence gave the place an altogether eerie feel.

Using my shiny new map seemed to be working nicely and after a while, I decided to take one of the smaller roads. On the map it was just a tiny dotted white line. I'm not an off-roader by any stretch of the imagination and the bike is big and my legs are small, so I stopped at the turning and looked down the track before committing.

'Well,' I said, patting the tank, 'what do you think?'

With no complaints from the bike, I made my decision. 'You only live once.'

At first, it was easy and wonderful. Riding on my own in the middle of the Romanian Carpathian mountains brought out all my man feelings and it was all I could do to stop myself from beating my chest and shouting like Tarzan. I was in awe of the place and in awe of myself for getting out there and doing it. It was a wonderful couple of hours.

Soon enough though, the track started getting diffi-cult. Then it started climbing, and then it really started climbing. I had to weave all over the place to continue but continue I did. Before long, it became apparent that I could be in trouble. The incline was so steep that if I made even the smallest of mistakes the bike and I would have bounced down the mountain for at least three hundred yards before stopping. The only choice I had was to continue.

'Jesus Christ Richard.' I was struggling for breath. 'Sure, it's a cool way to go but not aged in your forties.'

This went on for what was probably only half an hour, but it was incredibly hard work and bloody scary. I'm not exactly sure what I expected but when I eventually reached the top, I was disappointed to discover a scene of complete serenity. Families were enjoying picnics on a blanket of beautiful green grass with girly eco-friendly hatchbacks sitting proudly next to them. There was even a friend-ly-looking cow grazing lazily on the succulent pasture.

My manly prowess went from Rambo (First Blood) to
My Little Pony (Pink and Fluffy Edition) in less than the
time it took to write this sentence.

'How the…?' I said, breathing heavily from the ascent.

I was covered in a thick layer of sweat and can't have
smelt terribly good but that didn't stop a number people
from coming over to talk.

'Wow! We thought that road was closed,' one lady said.

'Completely impassable,' said another.

My prowess was hanging in tatters, but I recovered
slightly and listened intently after hearing that. It turned
out that there were two ways to get to the top. One was
to take the nice and easy, meandering dirt road which had
a few bumps but not a great deal more. The other was to
simply, and I quote 'ride straight up the side of the bloody
mountain!' It seemed I'd taken the latter choice and we all
laughed at my misfortune.

'When you make your way down from here you enter
into Transylvania. You need to be very careful,' said one
of the women. I thought she was joking

'Vampires?' I replied.

'Nope. Bears.'

I thought I may have offended her with my silly vampire
comment but if I had, she didn't let it show. She insisted
on telling me a story about a good friend of hers who was
attacked the year before last.

'She was silly,' she said, 'walking alone in the evening.'

Her face was deadly serious. Her partner was equally

as serious and joined in with the odd nod here and there.

'She was found by a car driver with half her scalp ripped off.'

Her partner spoke only in Romanian and I couldn't understand exactly what he said but it was plain he wanted her to stop. She didn't.

'She needed more than 200 stitches in her head and 60 in her arm and hands. She's now recovered but she's not the same.'

'I'm sorry to hear that,' I said, feeling a little uncomfortable.

'Be careful.'

And that was the end of the conversation. They turned away and I walked back to my bike.

When I said I was going to get a motorbike licence and a nice big bike, I was told I'd crash and die. When I said I was going to ride my motorbike to Morocco through the edge of the Sahara, I was told I'd be mugged and killed. These stories were easy to ignore; they were from people who didn't have a motorbike licence and hadn't visited such places. They were scare stories and didn't work on me. The story of the bear attack, however, was different. It was from someone who'd had real experience and that made a difference. That made me listen.

My ride down the mountain was far less eventful than my ride up. The gradient was slight, and the surface was reasonable. There were a few bad areas, but the heavy bike handled them with ease. In the time it took me to get down I only saw three cars, all travelling in the opposite direction. It was a pleasant ride but in the back of my mind were the bears. I knew the chance of actually being attacked while riding a noisy motorbike in the daytime was almost non-existent, so I wasn't too worried. When I pulled over for a pee, surrounded by silence in the thick of the forest, I couldn't help but look around like a madman. The feeling of not being at the top of the food chain returned, and I didn't like it.

Once down the other side, the combination of some hard riding, the hot weather and forgetting to eat gave me a bout of the wibbly wobblies. I'd done okay mileage-wise and decided that riding straight to Cârța, where the Transfăgărășan Pass begins, would be a good idea. The ride there was stunning in a very Romanian kind of way.

I arrived at my campsite just outside Cârța at about eight. As I entered the field, I spotted a group of fellow Transalp riders. There was no need to carry out the usual lap of the site to find the best place; the spot next to them was available. The group were from Poland and had come to ride the Transfăgărășan Pass. With introductions done and Facebook friend requests accepted, I set about the important task of setting up camp. With time still on my side, I grabbed some clean clothes and took a much-needed shower.

Smelling of soap and shampoo, I then wandered off to find food. Unfortunately, the closest shop was some distance away which would have meant mounting up again. I quickly decided that was out of the question and returned to my tent for a rummage through my panniers.

'Oh, what a find.'

I extracted a half-eaten and hairy sausage roll and a packet of cheese and onion crisps. Not exactly fine dining but it would keep me alive until the morning. As I wiped fluff away, one of the Transalp riders came over with a large slice of pizza. I thanked her graciously and wished I had more to offer in return.

After a couple of hours writing my blog, I climbed into my sleeping bag and quickly drifted off to sleep. My day's route included the following places: Campsite (Demelza), Ciocăneşti, Iacobeni, Argestru, Vatra Dornei, Plaiu Şarului, Panaci, Coverca, Bilbor, Secu, Topliţa, Gălăuţaş, Sărmaş, Gheorgheni Gyergyószentmiklós, Secuieni, Vânători, Albeşti, Sighişoara and finally the campsite just outside of Cârţa.

Mileage for the day was 245 miles, bringing the total for the trip so far to 2,608 miles.

DAY TEN

MONDAY, 26TH JUNE 2017

What A Monday!

WOKE UP feeling nice and fresh after a solid night's
sleep. I didn't hang around as the Transfăgărășan Pass
was waiting and I was excited. After a large, strong
coffee I packed everything up. My friendly biker neighbours gave me a Romania sticker for my bike, which was
very nice of them. We exchanged contact details and took
some more photographs, then said our farewells.

The riding and the weather were pure perfection. The
roads were exciting, and the views were to die for. The first
couple of hours were chock-a-block with photograph stops;
I'd ride around a bend and be presented with a view so good
that I had no choice but to stop and record it for prosperity.

'This is the one, just look at that! You'll never see another
view like that as long as you live.'

I'd then pull over and stop, turn the bike off, climb off,
remove my gloves, remove my helmet, unzip my jacket,

unzip the tank bag, find the camera, take the photograph, check it was okay, put the camera back into the tank bag, zip the tank bag up, zip my jacket up, put my helmet back on, put my gloves back on, get back on the bike, start it up and ride off.

Then a couple of hundred yards later I'd repeat the process. After a while it became such an ordeal, I began muttering 'not another bloody vista' round almost every bend.

It didn't take long to realise that the entire place is one giant photo opportunity. With a load of photographs under my belt, I was really able to enjoy the Transfăgărășan Pass. As the road climbed, I found myself waiting for the inevitable loss of power from the bike, but it never happened. The premium fuel I'd been using made all the difference and even at the highest point, when the GPS was indicating almost 6,700ft, the bike remained strong with no sign of weakness whatsoever.

About halfway through the pass was a rather eerie looking tunnel cutting through the very top part of the mountain. As I approached, the black hole of the entrance got bigger and bigger. The lights inside showed the tunnel descending steeply downwards, probably into the depths of a dark and scary netherworld.

As I rode past the metal shutters beside the entrance, it felt like I was entering some kind of mine shaft. Once inside the noises from the bike and other vehicles produced a deep, resonating rumble which, when combined with the huge temperature drop, only increased the feeling of it all being quite wrong. Seeing the small, white dot at the other end was very welcome and soon enough I was spat out the other side and back into the bright light of the real world.

My eyes adjusted to the daylight and revealed the most incredibly beautiful surroundings. I rode on in awe for another few miles and it just got better and better. When my senses could cope no longer, I pulled over and made a coffee, revelling in my situation. That's when I realised it was, in fact, Monday morning.

This, I decided, was a photo opportunity not to be missed. I found my pad and drew 'MONDAY MORN- ING!' onto one of the pages. I rummaged around and found my tripod.

As I've already mentioned, my camera has the most incredibly complicated self-timer, so it took a good 20 minutes of farting around to get a photograph. About five seconds before the photo was taken a car drove past. The lady within saw the sign and shouted.

'Monday morning!'

We both then screamed 'aaah!'—which is when the camera took the photograph.

I continued through the Transfăgărășan Pass thor- oughly enjoying the best Romania had to offer. All the bikers waved. Even a Porsche driver who flew past me at God only knows what speed stuck his arm out of the window and said hi. It was 'one of those times' in 'one of those places'—where you can't fail to be happy. More than once I stopped, turned around and rode back for a few miles just to prolong the pleasure.

As I descended to the lower altitudes, I noticed groups of people gathered around various places at the side of the road. I stopped to see what was going on. It turned out that water pipes poking out of the side of the mountains at these lower altitudes deliver the most exquisite water to anyone who wants to stop with a container.

'It's the best water anywhere in Romania,' one lady told me.

Going by the fact there were about 20 people queueing and some of them had as many as five large containers to fill, I didn't doubt her. I had to try some for myself so returned to the bike and removed the four Sigg water bottles and Thermos flask.

It took a while to reach the front of the queue, so I made the most of it, filling everything I had, drinking a load and filling them again. No one seemed to object; in fact, everyone was not only content with waiting, but they were actually enjoying the moment. With absolutely zero chance I'd made a mistake and filled up with carbonated water I rode off happy in the knowledge I would enjoy—and not endure—my evening coffees from now on.

Next on the list was the Transalpina Pass, further to the west. I plotted a route using my map and headed off full of incredible memories of the Transfăgărășan. No wonder the chaps from Top Gear called it the world's best road.

With all the excitement I'd completely forgotten about fuel but luckily, a large petrol station jogged my memory. I glanced at the gauge to find I had no fuel. None. I rode into the station and filled my thirsty and abused bike up with super-mega 102 octane premium jet fuel.

When I entered the shop to pay, I realised how ravenous I was and stocked up with a deep-fill chicken and stuffing sandwich, a peppered steak slice, a premium Cornish pasty and a rather cheap-looking but utterly irresistible pork pie. I also bought some more water and enough fresh coffee to sink the Titanic/fill up my now empty flask.

My plan was to ride to somewhere beautiful and quiet and enjoy my food but immediately I exited the shop, I was joined by a rather unkempt old girl I'm sure was a Golden Retriever in a previous life. She looked up with gorgeous doggy eyes.

'Come 'ere you,' I said, kneeling down.

She slowly, reluctantly came over and allowed me to fuss her.

'I'd say we've got ourselves a change of plan wouldn't you, little one?'

With the dog in tow, I pushed the bike to the deserted far end of the station and sat down. My hungry friend kept her eyes fixed on mine. When I gave her some more fuss, her tail twitched and we both knew we were mates.

The food I'd bought was halved; every time I ate, the dog ate too. In between scoffing our food down, I gave my new friend lots of fuss and told her stories about my travels so far. After we'd shared the pork pie, I told her about my doggy at home. I couldn't find a bowl anywhere so I cut one of the water bottles in half and held it so she could drink. She drank about half a litre of water before stopping. She must have been a very thirsty girl.

As a dog owner, you believe you can tell the difference between a dog that has grown up on the streets and a dog which was once a cherished member of a family. I was about 80 per cent sure that this dog was the latter. That changed to 100 per cent when she lay next to me, put her head in my lap and closed her eyes. I sat for another ten minutes drinking coffee with her head still in my lap. She seemed to sense when I'd finished as she stood up and walked out of the station, around the corner and disappeared.

As I got closer to the Transalpina Pass the road began to climb, and then climb further. Soon I was back up at 3,500ft. The temperature was hot, the air was saturated with humidity and the sky was looking very dark and angry. It was going to rain and if I didn't find somewhere to stay soon, I would get very wet indeed. I pulled over and quickly asked the GPS to find a campsite. The answer was about 50 miles in the direction I was heading. I jumped on the bike and sped off toward an ever-darkening sky.

As I journeyed to my salvation, the sky got darker and angrier. Finally, eight miles off the campsite, it could hold on no more and the heavens opened. To call it rain is to do nature an injustice. It came down with such force that attempting to keep dry was completely futile. Visibility had reduced to no more than a few feet, so I slowed right down. I'd closed all my flaps and vents but was still getting soaked. I became conscious that my arse was wet and there was an immense flash, a deafening crack and a strong smell of burning.

'Fucking hell!'

My instant reaction was to throw my head forward and press down onto my petrol tank in a kind of cringe. I've always found thunder and lightning fascinating, but this was different, and I was not just scared—I was terrified. You really can't appreciate the raw power of nature until you've witnessed it right there staring you in the face. It dominates with such completeness that any feelings of insignificance disappear into, well, insignificance. As I was so high up, the only thing higher than my highly conductive head were a few telephone cables. With the weather doing its level best to use the air as a conductor I found myself repeating expletives over and over again.

With the sky full of electricity and the rain continuing to hammer down, I pulled into the campsite and rolled up to reception. Getting off a bike in soaking wet leathers is a horrible experience but I was so pleased I'd made it to safety without being struck by lightning that I didn't even notice the discomfort. I was offered a place for my tent quite out in the open or my very own mini villa, which I immediately opted for.

I pushed my bike to my little villa and retreated inside. I stripped off completely to dry myself from head to toe, put on a fresh set of clothing and sat by the door to watch the hammering rain and plan the blog. Soon the rain slowed, then stopped. The heat of the day was subsiding but still strong enough to turn the downpour into a thick, low mist. The sound of dripping water from outside made my accommodation even cosier and I was excited at the prospect of sleeping in a real(ish) bed.

With the blog plan pretty much complete I ventured off to find the restaurant. It was very small and had a personal feel to it. I was given a handwritten menu by the young son, then an explanation of the dishes on offer. I opted for a typically Romanian dish, half a large fish I'd never heard of with mashed potato and lemon. It was delicious.

Stomach full, I was keen to write. When I reached the villa, I found the local stray positioned outside. It was as if the Golden Retriever had telephoned and told him what to expect. Luckily, I still had some leftover food in my pannier, so this was duly removed and given to the little fella. When one of the owners saw me feeding and fussing the dog, he came over and told me his name was Bob.

The next two hours were spent writing and scratching myself. Going by the lumps on my arms and legs, I'd say I'd been given a damned good going over by a pack of hungry horseflies. I tried as best I could not to scratch but sometimes it would all get a bit too much and I'd go mad for a few minutes and give them hell. I don't normally have too much trouble with bites, but I'd used my beautifully scented girly liquid soap during my last shower and, as nice as it was, I think it was a huge come-on for the horse-flies. I decided it was probably best to stink for a while.

Once my blog was done, I slipped into what felt like the most comfortable bed in the whole world and thought about being crossed by those villagers and then almost being struck by lightning. Of course, it was just a coincidence. Wasn't it? I closed my eyes and slipped off to sleep.

The route had been a simple one. From the camp-site just outside of Cârța, I made my way south on the 7C, otherwise known as the Transfăgărășan Pass. From there I headed in a westerly direction, got hopelessly lost and somehow ended up on the 7A. My mini villa for the night was a few hundred yards from where the 7A joins the 67C, about half-way up the Transalpina Pass.

Mileage was 196 miles, bringing the total for the trip so far to 2,804 miles.

DAY ELEVEN

TUESDAY, 27TH JUNE 2017

A Long Day In The Saddle

AFTER A superb night's sleep in my almost proper bed, I woke feeling ready. I The rain and mist had disappeared, revealing another beautiful day.

'Another shitty day in paradise!'

My ears heard my own voice, but my brain heard my Dad's from my childhood. I smiled, grabbed my bag and made my way to the toilet block with the intention of having a morning pee and cleaning my teeth. I was confronted with an odour so strong I could actually taste it. I quickly exited and decided the nearby wooded area would suffice nicely.

At the villa, I put on fresh boxers, socks and a part-worn T-shirt in the hope my leathers would be at least reasonably dry. Thick leather is a wonderful material if you're sliding down the road on your arse or if you're trying to look like a 'too smooth to move' biker but after a good soaking it's crap. Not average, not poor but completely crap. My first thought as I climbed into my leather trousers was 'a little damp' but then I tried moving and squelched. Not the best feeling in the world. Without any other options it wasn't going to be the most comfortable ride but hey, it was a weekday and I was on an adventure, riding my motorbike through Romania.

'Stop your bloody moaning,' I said, taking in the wild, mountainous scenery.

Paid up and packed up, I swung my leg over the bike and plonked my bottom on the seat. I ignored the squelch like a proper man and rode out into the beautiful morning. I chuckled when my mind worked out that I was taking my bike up the Transalpina Pass. Now there's a phrase that should be cockney rhyming slang if I've ever heard one.

My original plan was to ride north through the pass, turn around and go back through it in the opposite direction. Then I'd continue all the way to Bulgaria. This sounded like a good idea while sitting in my warm bed but once I got underway all that changed. The combination of the altitude, time of day and my wet leathers meant it wasn't the wonderfully idyllic ride I was expecting. It was bloody freezing. Normally I'd have stopped to put on more clothes, but everything would just end up soggy, so I shivered and concentrated on the scenery.

It didn't take long for the rising sun and the descending altitude to warm the place up nicely. As I rode down the north end of the Transalpina Pass, I unzipped my jacket and let it flap around in the wind which dried it out surprisingly quickly. Unfortunately, my trousers took far longer to dry but with the relentless heat from the lower altitudes any remaining moisture stood no chance and they did dry eventually.

I wasn't expecting the ride to Calafat to be overly scenic but was pleasantly surprised when I found myself riding over stunning valleys, huge dams and full reservoirs. I pulled up, poured a cold coffee and fired off a few photographs. As I drank, I thought about my time in Romania and decided, there and then, that I would go back some day and do it justice.

At one point I was riding along a small winding road when I must have startled a flock of tiny birds. They took flight and, as luck would have it, went in my direction. For about ten seconds I was part of the flock. There must have been at least 20 little birds right next to me, which was amazing to watch from such close quarters. One even bumped into my crash helmet. It didn't take them long to realise we were going in the same direction and they flew away.

With the roads being so good and almost deserted, I made very good progress and soon the scenery changed. I rode through several places that initially felt like ghost towns. I stopped a few times to take photographs and found that people were actually living in the derelict remains of buildings. I decided it would have been wrong of me to take photographs of their not-so-fortunate situations so didn't get any. The one exception was taken because I didn't see any signs of life.

As I continued to the border, the GPS began making some very weird decisions. I'd be happily riding along on the main road, following the magenta line with the next turn miles ahead when, all of a sudden and without warning, it would change its mind and instruct me to turn off. From there it would proceed to take me through a load of tiny backstreets and alleyways, then put me back on the main road again, usually no more than a mile up the road.

Some of these detours would only take a minute or two but others were more than half an hour. I assumed the main road was blocked or closed for some reason and that GPS knew what it was doing, but after a particularly stupid detour traversing people's gardens, I decided to check it out. It wasn't blocked. I checked the GPS's settings, but everything seemed in order. These weird glitches continued throughout the journey and didn't do our already fragile relationship any favours, especially when the bloody thing started shouting 'TURN AROUND WHEN POSSIBLE!' over and over again.

As I approached the southwest corner of Romania, I found myself completely bogged down in traffic. With the temperature in the high thirties and dressed in my thick leathers, I was melting but there was little I could do so I just sat there and took it.

'It could be worse, old girl,' I said, rubbing my hand along the edge of the tank. 'I could be sitting in an office in Crawley.'

I thought about this for a while but whichever way I looked at it, Crawley seemed far preferential to my current predicament.

'Yeah, imagine that. Sitting in a nice air-conditioned office dressed in clean clothing enjoying my small slice of importance.' I paused. 'Sounds terrible.'

The traffic moved forward a little, then stopped. I noticed a chap in the car in front open his window and throw something out. It was a fast food bag. Then came some kind of container, a load of crumpled-up serviettes and finally a half-full cup. My initial thought was to post it back through his window but decided against it. Instead I got off my bike, walked over and picked up every last little bit of the litter. Once I was sure nothing was left, I went to a bin that was no more than 20ft away and popped it in.

I glanced at the culprit. He seemed very uncomfortable and refused to look at me, even when I walked right by his window. Without a single word being said, though feeling I'd successfully made my point, I returned to my bike. Two people in the car next to me clapped and smiled. I did a cool biker nod and smiled back.

When I'd entered Romania, I'd drawn out £100 worth of Romanian Leu. I'd spent a few of them but still had about £85 worth in my pocket. Knowing how notoriously difficult they are to exchange outside of Romania I was keen to spend them, and all I could think of was food, lots of glorious food.

I approached Calafat and the border with Bulgaria with this in mind and was looking for a nice restaurant or a supermarket. Before I knew it, I'd become side-tracked and arrived at the border. It was a proper one, with police, sniffer dogs, official-looking buildings and even the odd armoured vehicle. From what I could tell there was a queue for cars, a queue for trucks and a queue for me, which was empty. I half expected to be told to go back to the end of the car queue but to my amazement, I was approached by an official-looking chap who asked for my passport. Duly handed over, it was opened, closed and then handed back.

'Hit the road,' he said, smiling.

The first ten minutes in Bulgaria were spent on a fast, main road looking at dilapidated tower block after dilapidated tower block. Many looked like they had fire damage. Even though some had actually began falling down, most of them still looked occupied. Many of the vehicles parked close by had broken windscreens and flat tyres. In the distance, I could see a huge fire with miles and miles of black smoke drifting off to the east. It wasn't a pretty welcome, but I held high hopes for the more rural parts.

With the sun almost touching the horizon and my backside, knees and back shouting to stop, finding somewhere to stay became a priority. Knowing that blindly following a road on the off chance it was going the right way was probably not the best method of finding a campsite, I pulled over. My map of Romania obviously didn't include Bulgaria, and my map of Europe included such a tiny Bulgaria that it might as well have not existed. When I attempted to tell my GPS, I was in Bulgaria it made some weird farting noises, then switched itself off. I poured a coffee, sat on the ground and leant against the bike.

'Well, old girl,' I said, 'Welcome to Bulgaria.'

The time spent sitting in front of my computer looking at Google Maps seemed like 100 years ago but surprisingly, even idiot Georgiou could remember some of it. With Serbia a few miles west, I knew I had to head in a south-easterly direction towards Sofia, then head south. I removed my compass from my tank bag and found a bearing.

As the sun dipped below the horizon and its leftover glow slowly disappeared, the next 100 miles or so were pretty and I should have enjoyed it more. That that I'd not been able to find a place to stay was playing heavily on my mind. I'd tried the GPS again, but it said there were no campsites or hotels in the whole country. I tried my mobile phone, but it had no reception. My big plan was to ride to Sofia and hope I could find a hotel, but I wasn't sure how far Sofia was, so I started eyeing up laybys and pieces of rough ground at the side of the road.

During the next 20 minutes, I stopped three times thinking I'd found my ideal spot. The first one seemed quite good from a distance. It was a deep layby with a grassy verge hidden from the road. I rode up close and shone the bike's headlight in its direction. Close up it didn't look so great. There was rubbish everywhere and then I spotted a poo on a bed of toilet tissue.

'Please tell me that's not human,' I mumbled in disbelief.

I didn't really believe it could be, so foolishly leant forward for a closer look. I shall refrain from explaining what I saw in great detail but suffice to say it was indeed human. I concentrated on keeping my coffee down.

'You have to be kidding me. That's shit, that's what it is.'

I let out a little laugh. If sleeping there was my best option, I would ride through the night. I was not going to bed down with another person's poo.

The other two possible spots I found also contained lots of rubbish and toilet tissue. I gave them a very wide berth and did not examine too closely. Resigned to the fact I was indeed going to be ride through the night, I carried on. I checked my fuel gauge as I spotted a petrol station up ahead. There were no fancy fuels in this place. The choice was simply petrol or no petrol. I opted for the petrol.

Inside the shop was a fine selection of food on-the-go. I chose a sandwich, a tub of cold chicken and a packet of crisps and found a map of Bulgaria. The bubbly check-out girl was very chatty and we talked for a while about my trip and her road trip around Romania. I told her about my weird experience of being crossed by the locals, then nearly being struck by lightning. She said some Romanians are very religious and may have taken offence by the big bike on a Sunday morning.

'They also don't like skaters and women who don't wear bras,' she added.

This really made me laugh. How random was that? I rode away with a happier outlook, but it didn't take long before I started worrying again. Just as I was giving up hope of finding somewhere for the night, I stumbled across a lovely-looking place with a sign outside that read 'restaurant and hotel'.

'Aaah,' I said, almost dribbling in my helmet. 'Aaah... please, please, please.'

I could see some lights still on in the main building so grabbed my stuff and went to investigate.

'Do you have a room?' I asked.

'Of course we have a room,' came the oh-so welcome reply.

I was shown where I could put my bike and taken to my room. It looked very posh and my mind wondered how much it was going to cost. Before I could ask, I was told the room was 15 Euros. Wow! Cheaper than many of the campsites I'd been staying in.

It was heavenly. I stripped off, jumped in the shower and stayed there for at least 20 minutes, feeling the aches and pains of a very long day in the saddle wash away. Cleanly shaven and feeling fresh, I made a coffee, sat on the bed and wrote my blog. Tired from the almost 16-hour ride, I had it uploaded in under an hour.

This had been the route. From my campsite in Obârşia Lotrului I went north on the 67C covering the top half of the Transalpina Pass. I then went through the following places: Petreşti, Turmaş, Tămăşasa, Călan, Băţălar, Haţeg, Bucova, Glimboca, Sadova Veche, Rogova and Calafat, where I crossed the border into Bulgaria. From there I went through Vidin and Bela and finally ended up in a nice hotel about 20km north of Sofia.

Mileage for the day was 404 miles, bringing the total for the trip so far to 3,208 miles.

1. Parked up for the ferry crossing to Calais.

2. The photographic stretch of the D76.

3. Le Champ! I couldn't resist this photo opportunity.

4. The bike struggled with some of the dizzy heights of the Furka Pass, the Grimsel Pass and the Susten Pass but didn't let me down.

5. Carbonated coffee!

6. The ride from Lehota to Brezno was sublime with stunning views of the Slovakian Carpathian mountains.

7. Crossing the river Tisa.

8. Riding on my own in the middle of the
Romanian Carpathian mountains.

9. This cow was enjoying grazing at the top of a mountain.

10. Another remote route, this time on the look-out for bears.

11. Friendly Polish biker neighbours at a campsite just outside of Cârța.

12. One of the many amazing views on the Transfăgărășan Pass.

13. This tunnel on the Transfăgărășan Pass felt like a mine shaft.

14. Monday Morning!

15. My luxury mini villa a few hundred yards from where the 7A joins the 67C, about half-way up the Transalpina Pass.

16. Bob the local stray.

17. The ride to Calafat was stunning.

18. The derelict remains of a house. Some of the villages I passed were like ghost towns.

19. Verges dotted with wildflowers.

20. Another coffee break!

21. The steps down to the beach. This was day 13 of the trip.

22. The incredible formations at the Meteora.

23. Riding along the small roads was wonderful.

24. A sweaty selfie.

25. A delicious meal in Makrinitsa.

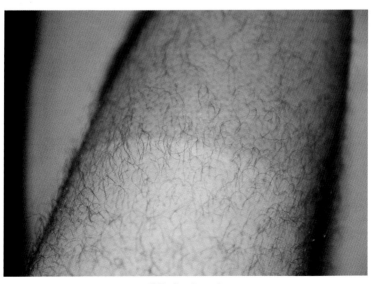

26. Sunburn!

27. The harbour at Chorto.

28. Another beautiful view!

29. A pretty woodland walk in my flip-flops. What could go wrong!

30. The steps I sat on to rest a while.

31. Mamma Mia!

32. Flowie and I, and Carl and Frances on our boat trip.

DAY TWELVE

WEDNESDAY, 28TH JUNE 2017

Mistakes, Mistakes and Laughing Like Never Before

WOKE UP in a very comfortable bed, in a very comfortable room, in a very comfortable hotel in Bulgaria. The whole vibe of waking up in a nice hotel room was completely different from a tent. All forms of hardship were missing, leaving only the pleasures like my own bathroom, running water, electricity, a fresh coffee machine and a body that didn't feel like it had slept on the floor for the first time in weeks.

After my morning ritual of toilet and teeth, I grabbed my map of Bulgaria and returned to bed. I spread it out in front of me but couldn't seem to get my head around it. A few moments later, and to my amusement, I realised I had it upside down. Without the benefit of the English alphabet it was difficult to know. Unfortunately, in my haste I'd bought a map that only showed place names in the Cyrillic alphabet, but I did my level best to plan a rough route through the rest of Bulgaria to Greece.

Most of the time I used fast main roads to make my way south but when I used the smaller roads, I noticed how the sides were dotted with wildflowers. The combination of the slow speeds and those beautiful wildflowers made riding a real pleasure. The heat though was always there, pressing down like the threat of something bad. Every time I stopped it was a race to get my jacket, gloves and helmet off before I overheated.

Whenever I go on one of these journeys, I promise myself that I will wear all my protective gear all the time, but I always end up riding without my jacket or gloves when it really gets hot. I've never been caught out and crashed without my gear on, but it is a risk. The last thing any biker wants is to end up sliding down the road in just a T-shirt grating one's skin down to the bone as you go. I'm very aware of this and do wear my jacket most of the time. But sometimes, well. Sometimes I bend the rules.

I tied my jacket to the back of the bike, put my gloves in the tank bag and rode along slowly on the almost car-less roads, enjoying the feeling of freedom that comes with riding in a T-shirt. Pottering along at between 20 and 30mph also had the added benefit of not being too noisy which was a nice break from the continuous loud drone from my helmet at sixty.

Before I got back onto the fast roads I stopped and put

my jacket and gloves back on. My plan was to visit the Rila Monastery on the way but as I turned off towards it, it became apparent that the place was going to be a complete tourist fest at the end of a painfully long queue. I decided against it and continued southwards towards Greece.

When I reached the border, I rode past all the cars and trucks right up to the front, which seems the thing to do if you're on a motorbike for some reason. The border police chap walked over and asked for my passport. He opened it, glanced at it for a second or two, closed it and gave it back.

'Welcome home,' he said, smiling.

I smiled back, thanked him and rode into Greece. As I left the border, I remembered about my pocket full of Bulgarian Lev. I'd drawn out about £100 worth and had hardly spent any of it. Just like when leaving Romania, my plan was to spend them all before crossing the border. Just like Romania, I forgot.

'Bugger. Looks like tonight's meal will comprise of about £85 worth of Romanian Leu for starters and about £85 worth of Bulgarian Lev for mains.'

Knowing that both these currencies were difficult to change outside of their respective countries I shook my head, amazed by my own stupidity—again. But for some reason, I felt like the pressure was off. Romania and Bulgaria were completely new to me and as such, I felt like I needed to be alert and struggled to relax. Greece, on the other hand, felt reasonably familiar and, as well as being my ancestral homeland, I'd been on many a holiday around the islands. I relaxed and followed the road knowing everything would be fine.

I followed the road with a new-found confidence, believing it actually wanted to take me the right way. I'm not sure if I was surprised when I arrived at a military base. I was confronted by two camo-clad soldiers armed with what looked like a nice set of G3 rifles. Before I could climb off the bike and apologise, they had opened the gate to the base and waved me in. I rode in and stopped. As I climbed off my bike and removed my helmet, the two young soldiers walked over. They didn't seem too concerned by my arrival; in fact they seemed relaxed and happy for me to be there.

'I'm completely lost. I have no map and my GPS is determined to kill me,' I said, stating the truth as I understood it.

It probably wasn't the best opening line, but it seemed to do the trick. One of the soldiers held out his hand and said hello while the other found a map. He pointed to various roads. With the pointy end his military calibre rifle pressing against my leg (nope, that's not a euphemism), concentrating on the map was more difficult than I imagined. I did my best and soon had a picture of where I needed to go in my mind. They wished me the best of luck and I rode off towards Thessaloniki.

As I got closer to Thessaloniki the roads got bigger and the petrol stations more impressive. I filled up with the top-spec premium stuff and made my way inside to pay.

After finding a decent map of Greece, with English and Greek place names, I joined the long, slow-moving queue. The teller girl insisted on talking to everyone she served. It was amusing to watch people battling between being polite and getting away. I was pleased to note that everyone opted for polite, however, I could also feel the frustrations of those around me.

When I reached the front, I paid safe in the knowledge I could only speak English.

'Thank you,' I said, 'and have a nice day!'

'Oh, you're English!' she replied, and made herself comfortable by leaning against the counter.

There was a cough from behind, definitely a prompt for me to get a bloody move on. I had a choice. Should I go down the polite route or just bugger off?

'Yeah, I'm on a motorbike trip,' I said, putting my gloves and GPS on the side, indicating to the cougher that I might very well be some time. 'I've ridden here from England and I'm meeting my wife and friends in the Pelion in a week's time.'

For a moment she seemed stunned into silence, but I soon realised that she just had so much to say that she didn't know where to start.

'We're going to have a heatwave,' she informed me. 'It's going to be in the mid-forties—maybe even hotter.'

We chatted but before long the grunts and coughs won me over and I left happy that I'd done the polite thing. I thought about how hot it was already and what it would be like in the mid-forties. One of my friends had already told me about the heatwave and now with two people having told me, it became a little more real, and a little more daunting.

I pushed the bike to the corner of the petrol station and retrieved my new map of Greece. I was somewhere north of Thessaloniki and wanted to head south towards to the Pelion. I picked a place to head for. Kato Sotiritsa was my destination for the day.

I waited patiently for the GPS to produce a route. When it finally revealed one, I let out of big sigh and shook my head. As the crow flies, Kato Sotiritsa was about 120km away, but the GPS wanted me to take me a weird route inland totalling 370km! This was not right. I started checking the settings for something obvious. It didn't take long to find that the GPS was set to avoid toll roads. Yeah, I'm a tight git. Once this was corrected the route settled down to a much better 170km.

I tried my hardest to keep track of where I was but with my terrible sense of direction, I was soon out of my depth and blindly following the GPS's magenta line. I noticed I'd gone around Thessaloniki and was heading south and that was good enough for me.

With no mishaps or wrong turns for the best part of an hour, my confidence grew. Needless to say, it wasn't long before I'd experienced one of my special 'Richard Georgiou' moments. The GPS asked me to turn off the toll road in five kilometres, four, three, two, one and… I got side-tracked and missed my turning. I was irritated to find my only choice was to go up the toll road for 20km, turn around and ride the 20km back to the turning I had missed.

After a few choice expletives, I accepted my fate. I did as I was told and pulled up at the toll station. I then rode around a few roundabouts to another pay station, where a nice-looking young lady took some more money from me. I then got back onto the toll road and set off for another 20km back to the missed turning. I concentrated really hard.

'Just pay attention you idiot. Adults do it all the time. Be a big boy. You've got this.'

I kept a close eye on the GPS. Five kilometres, four, three...

'Come on fella, you can do it.'

...two and one. When the GPS reading said 600 yards, I looked up the road and saw the turning. I concentrated harder and turned off.

And then realised in horror that I'd turned off 300 yards too early and that I had no option but to ride the 20km back up the toll road. Again.

The string of expletives was fired out with real vigour but there was no point in throwing a wobbly. I calmly rode the 20km up the toll road, again, and stopped at the first pay station. The chap smiled knowingly and took more money. I made my way around the roundabouts and stopped at the next pay station to get back on. The girl took one look and pissed herself laughing.

'You're back!'

We had a bit of a laugh at my expense and I buggered off feeling like the idiot that I was.

'See you in a minute!' I shouted.

I rode the 20km back down the toll road and as my turn off got closer I concentrated like I'd never concentrated before. I counted down the kilometres, then the metres. I passed the wrong turn I'd taken earlier, then realised there was no other turning. Just at that moment, the GPS piped up.

'Take the turning. Take the turning.' Pause. 'Turn around when possible.'

'Fuck off!'

I switched the bloody thing off and decided to ignore it forever; I would use my brain and eyes and follow the road signs. A few kilometres down the road I found another turning that looked much better. I was taken around a few sweeping bends then back onto the toll road. Rather sheepishly I switched the GPS back on to find, shock horror, that I was being taken 20km up the toll road for the third time!

That was it. I completely lost my temper. I fired out the most horrific set of vulgarities with such force I was surprised my tonsils didn't come flying out with them. My ranting and raving continued for quite some time but by the time I was halfway there I had accepted my fate. I could actually taste blood in my mouth after that particular tirade.

I'd calmed down by the time I'd reached the pay station and was seeing the funny side. The chap took my money again and let out of little laugh but did his best to remain professional. I then made my way around the rounda-bouts to the other pay station. The moment the girl saw me she had a complete fit. I could do nothing else but join her and we literally cried as we laughed. She told me the road layouts had changed a while ago and that many people made the same mistake. I, however, was the first to come back three times—which set us off again. She gave me a big hug, wished me well and laughed at me once more. I looked in my mirror as I rode off. She was standing there waving at me like an old friend—and still laughing.

On my way back to the dreaded turn offs, I decided I needed a plan. I pulled over onto the hard shoulder and examined the map, carefully noting names of the roads that I was looking for. I stuck them in the top of my tank bag where I could see them. I also told my GPS to avoid toll roads at all costs. This time I managed to take the correct exit and ended up on a wonderfully small road that wiggled its way south. There was a part of me that felt like getting off and kissing the ground, but I didn't.

After having spent such a long time on the toll road, riding along on the small roads of Greece was wonderful. Time had ticked on considerably and the sun was getting low in the sky, reminding me I needed to find somewhere to stay. I decided to ignore that and pulled over for a coffee. With the mountains in the distance, sunflower fields to both sides and a temperature that was not as oppressive as before, it was almost impossible to not to love this side of Greece. I could feel the stress in my body slowly ebbing away.

As I rode off, my jacket flapping in the wind, I reflected on the toll road episode and wondered how I consistently manage to be such an idiot. Other people make mistakes, but I manage to make them so often that I started to wonder if I have a bit of brain damage. Either I do or I'm just incredibly lazy. I decided that both were not just possible but probable. We've all got those 'I was dropped on my head as a baby' stories but I think I actually was. Perhaps I bounced on the lobe that controls directions and squished it a little. It would go some way to explain why I can't remember routes I've ridden or work out routes. Anyway, my all-important conclusion was that whatever my problem, it had resulted in floating around Greece on my motorbike while most people were working. I happily accepted my 'problems' as a part of my unique make-up.

The sun dropped lower in the sky as I made my way to Kato Sotiritsa but the atmosphere refused to cool. Instead it just got more and more humid. By the time I eventually arrived I was sweating profusely and very keen to find somewhere to stay.

The first four places I stopped at were full and the fifth was closed. Then I found a rather nice-looking hotel with lots of people milling around. I struggled into reception in my thick leathers, lugging my heavy tank bag and helmet.

With no air conditioning, the reception was baking hot and as sticky as hell. I was greeted by a young lady with black lipstick.

'Can I help you?'

'I'm looking for a room for the night.'

'Okay, we have a room for you.'

'Wonderful.'

I could feel sweat running down my back as I waited patiently for the receptionist to fill out a form with my details but then her mobile rang. As I melted, she chatted away in Greek, sometimes switching to English.

'Yeah, tomorrow at the tavern,' she said, laying back in her chair and laughing.

This went on for quite some time and I could feel my patience wearing thin. I glanced at another chap who was also waiting. I raised my eyebrows. He returned my smile and shrugged.

'No way,' she said into her phone, 'have you seen his car?'

After listening for 20 minutes, I lost my temper. I walked over to the photocopier and retrieved my passport, took the form and screwed it up and threw it on the floor. As I walked off, she came after me.

'Sir? Where are you going?'

'Where do you think I'm going?' I said, angrily. 'I'm going to find a hotel where the receptionist doesn't make me stand there for 20 minutes in a boiling hot room while she arranges her bloody social life.'

And with that, I about turned and left the building.

The sun was a fair bit lower in the sky. I looked at the map for another town close by, but nothing stood out, so I consulted the GPS. Apparently, there was a hotel 23km away. I followed the magenta line up into the hills and through tiny villages. If I wasn't in a bit of a pickle, I would have thoroughly enjoyed it but with the light fast disappearing, I was keener than ever to find somewhere to stay.

In one hilltop village, I rode into a tiny courtyard which had three little tracks out. The GPS had no idea what was going on, so I had no choice but to just pick one. I chose the left track and started down it. After a few hundred yards it narrowed considerably and became very steep. I continued down and down, and eventually came to a locked gate.

Now in a car you could reverse back up the track; it wouldn't be pretty, but you could do it. Motorbikes don't have a reverse gear so that was out of the question. As I saw it, I had three options.

Option one was to turn the motorbike around and ride it back out. Unfortunately, the track was narrower than the length of the bike. With some kind of long building to my left and a serious-looking fence to my right, there was no way to turn the bike around. I actually tried laying it down and lifting the front over the back but with a heavy bike and just one person, it was never going to happen.

Option two was to push the bike backward up the track. It was comprised of loose dirt and was both steep and long. I walked about 50 yards, looking for places I could turn the bike around but there were none. It was as if the place had been designed to capture idiots on motorbikes. And capture me it had.

Option three was to curl up into foetal position, stick my thumb in my mouth and cry like a baby. Instead I made a coffee and thought about what to do next. I examined the gate, but it was definitely locked and very solid. Beyond was a small house and I saw some movement.

'Hello there! You, I say. I'm in need of some assistance!'

When that didn't work, I called out a loud 'HEEEEELP!' This did the job perfectly. A couple came out to see what was going on, but they only spoke Greek and I only spoke English, which made things somewhat slow and frustrating. I hoped my position was obvious and that they would open the gate but after ten minutes of special sign language, I worked out that they didn't have the key. They then promptly disappeared inside their home without saying another word, closing the door behind them. I hoped they were getting something to help but after 20 minutes of them not reappearing I gave up. I poured another coffee.

'Okay bike, it's just you and me then,' I said, feeling completely beaten.

I chatted away to the only friend I had and congratulated myself on another fine mess I'd got myself into. I finished the coffee and was considering pitching my tent when I heard a vehicle. I looked up to see a very small, beaten-up car reversing toward me—and it had a tow bar.

It stopped about 80 yards away and a man climbed out with a long rope. He looked, laughed and then handed me one end of the rope. We did our best to devise a plan and, despite our different languages, conjured something up. I tied the rope around the end of my swing arm and he slipped his end over his tow bar.

'Slowly please,' I said, hoping this wasn't going to end badly.

'Slowly,' he repeated.

Very slowly, my rescuer inched along. With 80 yards of rope there was a considerable amount of stretch, so I was kind of pulled up in bounces. The bike would stay still then zoom backward, which made it very difficult to keep upright. Over the next 20 minutes, we managed to get the bike back up to a point where I could turn it around. It wasn't pretty but it worked, and I didn't drop it once. Operation over, he shook my hand and pointed me in the right direction. Daylight had disappeared and I was covered in a smelly layer of dirt and sweat, or as the mosquitoes call it, lunch.

I got back on the bike. The moving air felt good, but that fact it was dark, and I still hadn't found anywhere to stay was pressing down hard. I followed the magenta line as best as I could and eventually reached the building the GPS thought was a hotel. It was closed—and obviously hadn't been open for a number of years. I slumped forward and rested my head resting on the tank bag. I checked the GPS again, but accommodation was thin on the ground and miles away. It was time to find a piece of ground to pitch my tent.

It wasn't easy in the dark but after riding around in the hills I found a nice spot that was quiet, reasonably clean and a little way away from the road. Bingo! I started setting up camp and was promptly eaten alive by just about everything that could fly and most things that couldn't. The bugs were prolific and refused to leave me alone. Bearing in mind that my tent door had broken about 2,000 miles ago and therefore allowing the mosquitoes free rein, I decided that perhaps camping wasn't such a good idea after all.

It was easy making the decision to ride through the night, but I didn't know where I was going and each time I stopped to look at the map, the mosquitoes went mad. I decided to ride down the hillside and get as close to the sea as possible, then I'd attempt to read my map and plot a course somewhere. As I descended the hilltop, I noticed the stress disappear. It was obviously being caused by the unknown element of the situation, not the actual situation itself.

About ten minutes later I rode around a bend and was confronted by a hotel sign. I rode in on the off chance and saw happy guests eating food and chatting.

'I'm looking for a room for the night, or a floor, or a cupboard,' I said, not believing they would have anything.

'That's no problem, sir, we have a room for you,' came the most welcome reply, 'and we're still serving food if you're hungry.'

I parked my bike round the back, took my luggage up to my room and climbed into the shower. Once clean and fresh I had a bite discovery session which revealed the extent of the gluttonous mosquito feast. Every piece of skin that I touched screamed 'scratch me' which made towel drying a most irritating affair. Itching from head to toe, I went downstairs, ordered and thought about how wonderful life was.

I'd forgot to record the place names I travelled through during the day so didn't know the exact route, but here it is as I remember. From my nice hotel 20km north of Sofia, I rode south using mostly main roads with the odd exception. I crossed the border at Kulata and entered Greece, got lost and ended up at a military base. I then headed south, went around Thessaloniki, up and down a twenty kilometre stretch of toll road three times and headed south again on beautiful little roads with very scenic views. When I reached Kato Sotiritsa, I went up into the hills, got lost, rode down a small track and ended up stuck. After being rescued I blindly followed the magenta line on my demented GPS to a hotel that had closed years ago. Lady Luck then found me a hotel close to the beach.

Mileage for the day was 385 miles, bringing the total for the trip so far to 3,593 miles.

DAY THIRTEEN

Me, The Beach and My Book

AFTER THE previous day's escapades, I felt I deserved a break so had a lazy start. I woke early, made coffee and sat on the balcony. The back cover of The Girl in the Spider's Web and the first few pages was all it took to draw me in. I decided, there and then, to stay a little longer.

Downstairs, my friendly host Dimitris presented me with a full continental breakfast, which set me up perfectly for the day and I booked the room for another night. With my camera, book and a bottle of water, I walked down to the beach. Wow! Not only was it beautiful, it was deserted and all mine.

Knowing how good I am at getting lost I looked for landmarks and made a mental note of my location. I then took photographs of the stairs back up to the hotel, just in case. The next four hours were spent walking a few miles in both directions, relaxing and taking photos. I walked on the edge of the water, a rare treat for my feet after being stuck in motorcycle boots for almost two weeks. It was wonderful and in all that time I only saw three people.

As the temperature increased, I ran into the water and swam around. After being cooked in my leathers for the last few days, bobbing around in the cooling water made a welcome change. Feeling I'd done the beach justice, I sat down on my bag and read, having swim every hour. Before I knew it, the afternoon turned into early evening and my stomach told me it was time to eat. The walk back took about 15 minutes and was quite strenuous. A combination of steep slopes and the heat and humidity made my legs a little wobbly but the thought of a plate full of fine Greek food and an ice-cold beer kept them moving.

After a long cold shower, I sat on the veranda, chose my food and opened my pad. This is what I wrote:

I'm writing this text from the veranda of the pension where I'm staying. The evening air is warm and humid, but the slight breeze keeps it pleasant. The roof is comprised entirely of vines, the beginnings of their fruits starting to appear. The gentle sound of Greek music is slowly replacing that of the cicadas as the sun makes its descent towards the horizon. The calamari starter is long gone, and I've just been presented with a beautiful-looking fillet of chicken accompanied by a full and glorious

Greek salad. Is it not moments like this that us Brits come here for? To my left is the road I rode in on. Though it has the comfort of familiarity, it's been done, enjoyed and lived. The road to my right is far more interesting. It represents opportunity and the excitement of the unknown. Tomorrow I take the road to my right, and who knows where that will lead. Perhaps new and exciting places. Perhaps.

ONE MAN ON A BIKE

DAY FOURTEEN

Cooked In Larissa And My Vindictive GPS

AFTER ANOTHER sound night's sleep in a real bed, I woke feeling fresh and ready for a little road trip. Before leaving home, my wife had told me about a huge rock formation in central Greece called the Meteora and her description had left a lasting impression. I wasn't keen to spend another day just chilling at the beach so decided to ride out and see it.

The plan seemed to make sense but for one exception: the heatwave was in full swing and the temperature was predicted to be in the mid-forties. Being tough, manly and stupid I dismissed this and with a plan in my head, I went downstairs for breakfast. As I tucked into scrambled eggs and toast, I noticed I'd forgotten to put on my shorts. I was sitting there in my boxer shorts which happened to be highly worn and not in the best condition. I continued eating and pretended to be a normal adult—something that didn't come naturally, but I think I managed to pull it off.

As I stood to leave, I noticed the button that held my fly closed had fallen off and I was not a million miles away from rudely pointing at the lady in front of me. I covered my dignity with my pad and casually made my way to my room.

I put on my leathers, grabbed my tank bag and made my way out to the bike. After walking around for a day in not much more than a pair of shorts and flip-flops, the leathers were a bit of a shock to the system. I was hit by the heat of the day. It was 9.30am and already 35 degrees.

It may have only been a day, but I'd missed the old girl. I swung my leg over her seat, hit the start button and tapped the gear lever. I'd already worked out my route and for once the GPS seemed to agree with me. As I saw it, the journey from my hotel to the Meteora was split into three parts. The first was getting to Larissa using small, twisty roads. The next part was going through, or rather around, Larissa. As Larissa was a reasonably sized city, I thought using the ring road was a fine idea and the GPS agreed. The last and final part was from Larissa to the Meteora along big, fast roads, which meant I'd be able to cover a decent chunk of the trip in good time. That was the plan anyway.

It went well until I had to slow down at a T-junction and it immediately became apparent the temperature was going to be a problem. I toyed with the idea of taking my jacket and gloves off but decided against it for the time being.

As I got closer to Larissa the traffic increased tenfold, then promptly stopped. Having chosen the ring road, I was hoping against hope that I'd keep moving but obviously hope wasn't enough. With the temperature sitting at 38 degrees I sat in the stationary traffic, melting.

After 20 minutes or so of almost no movement, I started feeling a little weird. I had to get out of the heat. I rode the bike up onto the pavement, removed my jacket, helmet and gloves and sat in the shade of a tree. After a long drink of water, I felt a bit better and realised the risk of dying from overheating in my leathers was higher than the risk of dying from a crash. That was all the excuse I needed. I tied my jacket to the back of the bike, stuffed my gloves in the tank bag and hoped it was going to turn out okay.

Ten minutes later I was back on the bike but without my jacket and gloves. I looked around at the traffic. For a ring road, it looked awfully like a city. The GPS had taken me right into the heart of the Larissa.

With the temperature now reading 39 degrees, the last thing I needed was to throw a wobbly, so I hated my GPS calmly, silently and completely, and continued. When the traffic stopped, which was often, I checked through the GPS's settings. For some reason, the route had changed from going around Larissa to going through it. I also found the settings had changed from fastest to shortest.

'That was not me!' I exclaimed. 'Bloody thing's got a mind of its own!'

I wondered if it was possible for a GPS to get a virus and came to the conclusion it had become possessed by a weird version of the Devil with a sense of direction even worse than my own. When I reverted the setting to fastest it told me to turn around when possible and became determined to take me back the way I had just come. I ignored its stupid route and continued west towards the Meteora.

Leaving Larissa was a pleasure. The road opened up and the traffic thinned out considerably. Without my jacket and gloves riding at 70mph felt both vulnerable and wonderful. Distance seemed to whiz by in no time and the memory of being stuck and cooked in Larissa became just another moment for my blog.

It wasn't long before I started to approach the town of Kalabaka. The traffic slowed but continued moving; a relief as the temperature sat at 41 degrees. I followed the signs and turned right before getting too far into town. I stopped a number of times to take photographs but couldn't help feeling that it wasn't quite what I was expecting. When I arrived at the place where all the famous photographs are taken, I stood there in awe at the incredible formations. The heat pressed down on me and tourists buzzed around, but in my mind, it was just me and the amazing geology.

I rode for an hour or so admiring the views and decided I wanted a Meteora sticker for my bike. I found a gift shop, rode between two giant coaches and parked up right outside. They had fridge magnets, postcards, calendars, T-shirts, skirts, tea towels, beach towels and even a wooden penis with pictures of the Meteora on—but no stickers. I found a chap to ask. He looked around but to no avail. I explained that it was to go on my bike, and he came out for a nose. It turned out he had studied economics in London a few years back and had ridden his nice and posh KTM all the way there from Greece. We had some bike talk and he gave me a fridge magnet as a souvenir. Nice chap.

With the heat zapping my energy my mind kept returning to the beach by my hotel. I left Kalabaka hoping I'd get back in time for a relaxing, and not to mention cooling, swim and a bit of reading.

The return ride back was nice and quick, and I was determined to use the ring road to get around Larissa. I kept a close eye on the GPS, but it behaved itself. I stopped at the side of the road just after Larissa for a drink of water and noticed the temperature was reading 46 degrees. I could feel every single one of them.

Dimitris was waiting at the hotel with a very welcome bottle of ice-cold water. What a host! He told me even the locals were finding the silly temperatures a struggle.

Once showered and changed I grabbed my book and water and went to the beach. I was surprised to find that, once again, I had the entire place to myself. I picked a spot, had a swim and sat down to read. Every 20 minutes or so I'd have another swim.

After a few hours of relaxing, I returned to the hotel for a meal and a bit of blog writing. As I ate chicken souvlaki and Greek salad, I thought about the coming few days. It was almost time to move on, but where to go?

I uploaded the blog and went on Facebook. One of my friends, travelling around the world on a little scooter, was going to be in the Meteora the following day. I thought about riding back there in the morning to see her but the idea of going inland again in those temperatures was unpleasant. In hindsight, I wish I had but there's always the next time. I sat on my balcony for a while, read and pondered over the options for the days ahead.

Mileage for the day was 165 miles, bringing the total for the trip so far to 3,758 miles.

DAY FIFTEEN

SATURDAY, 1ST JULY 2017

A Vegetable Patch And My Mountain Retreat

I WOKE EARLY feeling refreshed and ready to make a decision on the future of my trip. I spent quite a lot of time the previous evening mulling over my options so felt fully armed.

I would be meeting my lovely, and obviously forgiving, wife Flowie and four mates from the village in the Pelion on the 7th July, so I had a week to do whatever I fancied. The first option was to ride south and aim for a lap of Tripoli. If the weather was cooler, I would have definitely gone for this; however, with the heatwave in full swing and me struggling every time I slipped into my leather trousers, I decided it probably wasn't the best idea.

Option two was to ride to northwest and investigate the area. It was greener and more mountainous than the rest of Greece, which I liked the sound of. Unfortunately, this meant riding across the interior of the country in this immense weather, which I didn't fancy. I'd also be on the wrong side of Greece for meeting up with my wife and mates.

Option number three was to investigate the Pelion. This felt like the right choice. It was close, it was interesting and above all, I was pretty much there already. My plan was to pick a nice base for the week in a good location. I could then explore on foot while the heat persisted, then once it cooled down a little, I could go further afield using the bike and should I fancy a bit of pampering along the way, that would be fine too.

I searched the internet and found a number of possibilities. I've never really liked new stuff, instead preferring the character of older things. So, when I found the 'The Traditional Mansion—Evilion' I smiled and hit the booking button. It was located in the mountainside village of Makrinitsa, which looked like an interesting place in itself and an excellent base to explore from. For the almost bargain price of 270 Euros I secured it for seven days.

I made my way downstairs for breakfast. I was met by the ever-friendly Dimitris who served me with, among other things, my favourite: the humble boiled egg with soldiers and a tiny dish of salt. He joined me and we chatted about our respective lives but with time ticking on and the threat of another furnace of a day, it was soon time to depart. With photos taken and hands shaken, I jumped aboard the bike and set off towards the Pelion, and that was the end of my thoroughly enjoyable stay at Paradies.

My ride to Makrinitsa was only about 80km and for that reason, I assumed it would be an easy one. What a fool. I checked that the GPS was set to fastest route and to NOT use unpaved roads, then asked it nicely to work out the route to Makrinitsa. It gave me three options and I selected the one that said 49 miles. I checked the route against my map and found we agreed. We would be riding through Sklithro, Kalamaki, Kanalia, Glafira and then into Makrinitsa. It was definitely the scenic route with the smallest roads, but they were actual roads.

Riding along the small roads was wonderful, especially as the day hadn't really had much of an opportunity to warm up properly. With my jacket tied to the back of the bike, I popped along feeling the freedom one can only feel on a bike. The GPS directions all corresponded nicely with the map I'd stuck onto the top of my tank bag and all was well until I ended up in some chap's vegetable patch.

'Hmm, this doesn't look right.'

I couldn't work out where I'd gone wrong, but the GPS had switched itself to shortest route and ticked the use unpaved roads option. Bastard thing!

Correcting the settings, it instructed me to turn around when possible. Tiny Greek hillside villages don't lend themselves to following any kind of directions, whether from a map or a GPS, so I decided to just ride around and hope against hope that I'd find my way. As I struggled with the heavy bike the vegetable patch owner walked over and pointed up the hill to where I'd come from.

'Yes, sorry about this,' I said, gesturing at my GPS.

I managed to do a kind of eight-point turn all while being seriously frowned at by the unhappy man. I apologised once more and rode out of his garden.

After a few more wrong turns and map stops I somehow managed to get back on track and was heading towards Makrinitsa. All went well for a while until I reached a fork in the road. I could either take the left and continue on the main road or take the right, which looked smaller and a little hairy. It would have been an easy decision but for the fact that, according to my map, the main road went the wrong way. I took the right fork and hoped for the best.

At first it was exciting. The tiny road was quite steep with very tight hairpin bends and riding along in my T-shirt was fantastic. However, it wasn't long before it turned into a real handful. As the altitude increased the road got smaller and steeper. At one point I stopped and looked ahead in disbelief. The road had pretty much turned into a path, but it was the incline that grabbed my attention; it must have been 40 degrees. It would have been difficult even on foot but on a heavy bike, it was even more of a challenge. I got a run-up and zoomed up the path. At the top it twisted so sharply that I had to stop and allow the bike to roll back a little to get around. This went on for about 20 minutes and by the time I reached a proper road I was absolutely knackered and sweating profusely.

These tiny Greek village roads may be hard, but even on a heavy bike in this heat, they were lots of fun.

As I got closer to Makrinitsa I started getting a little worried that I'd made a bad choice as I could see no trace of life anywhere. The hotel was in a mountainside village far away from the beach, so I was relying on the village being nice with a selection of places to eat and perhaps a few shops to browse. If it wasn't, I was in for quite a miserable week.

Just as I was about to give up hope, the road name changed to Agios Georgiou and everything came alive. The views were to die for, streets turned to cobbles, old stone houses and shops had flowers outside and most importantly, it looked like there was a fine selection of places to eat, from your basic souvlaki all the way to fine cuisine. I bounced over the old cobbled road feeling the happiness that emanated from the people milling around. This was not only better than I'd expected, it was better than I'd dared hope!

When I'd made the booking, I noticed it said there was parking close by and as such, I was not expecting to park right next to the hotel. I rode as far as I could and when I could go no further, parked up with a load of other bikes. I unpacked and secured what was left then continued in the same direction on foot. It was hard work lugging all my stuff through the heat but knowing I was so close to a relaxing stay made it okay. I had no idea where I was going but that didn't matter for once, as a chap who was sitting drinking coffee with friends looked up and said: 'You must be Richard.'

Wow! Not only was the village beautiful, the hotel was perfect too. With its thick stone walls, heavy wooden doors and beautiful flooring, the place had ample character and fitted perfectly into the feel of the village. This was definitely for me. Lugging my stuff through a bustling village dressed in heavy black leather took its toll and by the time I'd reached my room I was about ready to collapse. I took a quick photograph of my horrible sweaty self and then jumped into a wonderfully cold shower, where I stayed for a wonderfully long time.

After a short nap to re-energise my poor, suffering body I decided to check out my new home. With my leathers replaced with shorts, T-shirt and flip-flops the slow walk around the village felt wonderful. In less than one hundred yards I found out that flip-flops on wet cobbles are bloody slippery. I also found out that when your arse hits the aforementioned cobbles it hurts and makes you feel really stupid (and it makes those around you laugh quite a lot).

The village was comprised of a very pretty central square with a huge tree to one side and chairs from a nearby restaurant to the other. Being on a hillside the views were exceptional. Just off the square was an old Greek Orthodox church with open doors and a cool, dark interior. The priest sat on a stone bench outside with a dog at his feet. The main drag, if you can call it that, was a narrow road just about wide enough for a very small lorry. A combination of restaurants and gift shops lined one side and on the other a view down the mountain to Volos. Most of the shops had flowers outside and the aromas emanating from the restaurants meant walking down the main drag was an aromatic affair. At the end of the main drag was a car park, then the road.

The unofficial parking place for bikes was at the join between the main drag and the square and to get to my hotel I had to walk through the square and up some cobbled pathways. Makrinitsa was a delightful place made even better by the fact that alongside the square was a small gully awash with fresh mountain water. The noise it made as it flowed past made it feel even more 'mountain village'.

I wandered down the main drag, about turned and made my way back, stopping at a restaurant that tickled my fancy. I ordered chicken souvlaki, Greek salad, an ice-cold bottle of mountain water and a Greek coffee and enjoyed my surroundings in the knowledge I now had a decent base to explore from.

I asked the waiter about the giant tree in the square and was told it was a bladanos tree and thought to be more than 1,000 years old. He also said it was probably the second oldest tree in Greece. I'm not sure if that's true but it certainly was huge.

With my stomach full of food and my veins full of coffee, I popped into the Greek Orthodox Church. I'm not religious in the slightest but I sat there and thought about my Grandad George for a while.

After a cold shower at the hotel, I made my way to the bar and was joined by the hotel's owner. We drank, chatted and laughed as the sun disappeared over the horizon and Volos shimmered below in the evening heat.

I returned to my room slightly inebriated, thought about what the coming days would bring, then drifted off to sleep.

My route for the day. From my hotel, I wiggled and wobbled my way through the following little villages getting lost for most of the way: Sklithro, Kalamaki, Kanalia, Glafira and Makrinitsa.

Mileage for the day was 56 miles, bringing the total for the trip so far to 3,814 miles.

DAY SIXTEEN

SUNDAY, 2ND JULY 2017

A Long Walk

WITH THE temperature predicted to be in the low forties it was definitely an 'explore on foot' day. Not wanting to be lugging too much around, I left my camera behind. I went to the bar to see what was available and admired the view of Volos as I enjoyed a breakfast of boiled egg, a slice of cake and a double espresso.

Outside I immediately noticed the heat. It was only about nine, but the temperature was already in the high twenties. I popped my sunglasses on and headed to the square. I'm not sure if it was the hour of the day or that it was a Sunday, but the village seemed even more tranquil than the previous day. The sound of bells from the church combined with the gentle trickling of mountain water running down the slipways completed the scene perfectly. I watched an elderly man watering flowers outside his shop and wondered about his life. I'm sure he had all the same problems and worries as the rest of us, but it was difficult to imagine as he tended his plants. After a liberal watering, he carefully checked the leaves and removed tired ones. When he finished with each plant, he ran his hand over the top like he was ruffling the hair of a young son.

I took in the sights and sounds as I went and was treated to a cornucopia of wonderful aromas from the restaurants; the sweet one was by far my favourite. I made a mental note to pop in on the way back. I passed gift shop after gift shop and peered into each one. Most sold the same stuff but one that sold baseball bats, which I thought a little strange. Then I saw handcuffs.

'Bloody hell, what kind of village is this?' I grinned.

I got to the end of the village and kept on going but with the temperature rising, I was a little worried about getting burnt. I don't tend to burn as a rule but in temperatures such as these, you never know. I'd attempted to buy sun cream the previous evening but unless you want a bead necklace, a wooden donkey or a fridge magnet, you're out of luck.

Being well aware of how terrible my sense of direction was, I concentrated on keeping my bearings and took a mental note of every junction and luckily there weren't many. Over the next three hours or so I ambled down the mountainside, and Volos got closer with every step. I followed the road for most of the way but once in a while, when there was an obvious shortcut, I'd cross some piece of dry ground then return to the road. Much of the road was pretty steep and I kept expecting my legs to start shaking, but for some reason they remained strong. When my ears popped, I turned around and looked up the side of the mountain to Makrinitsa and was surprised at the distance I'd walked.

I was hoping against hope that I'd stumble across a small café or bakery where I could indulge in cake and coffee but thus far, I'd been out of luck.

'Just another hundred yards,' I promised. 'There's bound to be one round that bend.'

After another hour I gave up. Walking back was hard work so I slowed right down and accepted it would take some time. I tried hard to remember the turnings I'd taken but I'm quite sure the route I took on the way up was different.

By the time I arrived back in Makrinitsa, the morning and most of the afternoon had disappeared. I was hot and sweaty and looking forward to a nice cold shower but as I passed the line of restaurants, the most glorious smells wafted out and I decided to pop in and investigate.

I pulled up a seat in the shade and when a waiter appeared with a wonderfully cold bottle of mountain water, I ordered pan-fried chicken. Between a bit of people watching and admiring the view, I read my book and enjoyed not being on my feet. With the heat being what it was, my appetite had all but disappeared but the moment my food arrived, it was back with vengeance. I had made an excellent choice. I then had a slice of cake and a double espresso to keep my caffeine addiction happy, before returning to the hotel for a shower.

All in all, I'd walked for some eight hours and was quite proud, especially considering the intense heat. The one thing that struck me was the complete lack of pressure; not once did I see anyone who looked to be in any kind of hurry. Everything was happening but at a pace far better suited to a hot environment. Perhaps I'm just used to living in a place where pressure and speed have become the norm.

I uploaded my blog, then spread the map out on the bed. As I ran my finger over a possible route for the following day, I noticed the silence. With the hotel's thick walls, air conditioning wasn't needed and so my room was silent. As I climbed into bed I hoped for a good night's sleep.

DAY SEVENTEEN

MONDAY, 3RD JULY 2017

Another Hair-raising Descent

TWO THINGS happened. The first is that I became a true devotee of my superb motorcycle and its incredible abilities. The second—my GPS and I are getting divorced. And yes, the two facts were linked.

I woke to the sound of incredibly loud cicadas rasping their racket through my window. I rolled over trying to get back to sleep when a 'loud and proud' rooster from hell started up.

'I'll give you cock-a-doodle-bloody-doo.'

I got up and had a shower.

Flowie was quite keen that I did a recce of the area where we'd all be staying when she and our friends arrived on Friday. I would ride to the villa she'd booked in Tsagarada and see what's what. I would take the low roads, skimming around the outskirts of Volos, and on the way back I'd take the high road through the mountains. And that, my friends, was the plan.

After a breakfast of scrambled egg and sponge cake, I rode off and checked my watch; it was 9am. The first 20 minutes went according to plan. Then the GPS asked me to take a left off the main road. I stopped and looked down the road in question.

'You have to be joking.'

The narrow track looked like the kind solely reserved for goats—incredibly steep and with a surface of loose stones and dirt. I decided to continue on the main road for a bit to see what happened.

The next road the GPS asked me to turn down looked much better, so I pulled over and checked the map. The road appeared as a tiny dotted line that seemed to be going in the right direction. With the map and my GPS in agreeance what could go wrong? It didn't take long to realise this track was punishment for not taking the earlier one. Within 100 yards it became so steep and narrow I was committed. I went around a slight right curve to find a van completely blocking my path. It had obviously been there forever as it had flat tyres and weeds growing through it. I managed to stop my bike on what must have been a 40-degree slope. Holding the front and rear brakes to stop it sliding, I wondered what to do. One thing was certain, the van wasn't going anywhere and, given it was the same width as the track, getting past was not an option.

To the left of the van was a house and to the right a bit of rough ground so steep and high it wasn't even worth considering. I let loose with my horn and waited.

Nothing.

'Hello!' I shouted, desperation in my voice.

Still nothing.

'Well, it looks like it's just you and me again, old girl. Sorry about this.'

I kept the back brake locked and slowly released the front just enough to allow me to steer to the right. I was hoping this would allow me to perform some kind of weird U-turn but instead, the bike just slid. I pulled the front brake but on the loose dirt the bike just continued and slid over the edge. In that horrific instant, realising I was going down 'the quick way', I found myself so consumed by terror that screaming even the simplest of expletives was impossible. Instead, I grabbed hard on the handlebars as we literally flew down the hillside.

To say it was messy would be an understatement of the most enormous proportions. We were hurtling down the hill completely out of control. We hit a hump in the ground and were immediately sent skywards. Moments later we landed with a bloody great clattering thud. Every bump sent us off in a different direction. After a particularly violent bump, I found us heading straight for the roof an old wooden barn. Just as I was resigned to end my days in the barn, the bike miraculously changed direction and we shot onto the road below. I grabbed for the brakes and skidded to a stop. I just about managed to get the side stand down before slipping off the bike onto the ground.

For the next few minutes, I sat there breathing heavily and feeling detached from reality. I was astounded that I was unscathed and hadn't come flying off in the thick of things. When I stood up, I was a little more shaken than I thought. My legs felt wobbly, but I ignored this as I checked the bike over. I expected to find quite a bit of damage but thankfully, other than a dent in the sump guard and a bit of plant life stuck in the rear brake calliper, all seemed well. It looked like the bike had got off lightly. Then I spotted that the tank bag was gone.

It contained my iPad, Nikon camera, mobile phone, wallet, passport and my all-important pad containing my scribblings from the journey. On wobbly legs I retraced my route as best I could and found it a few yards from where I'd come crashing over the first hump. Everything seemed okay but for a broken zip which refused to close; something I could live with.

Before setting off again I calmly removed the GPS from my handlebar and placed it in my tank bag. I knew I needed to head in an easterly direction so took a bearing from my compass, found a landmark and rode towards it.

With my 'event of the day' over, I hoped I could ride to Tsagarada without further mishaps. I felt and listened to the bike for any clues to damage but there were none. Everything seemed to be working nicely, with the exception of the top of my tank bag flapping around.

The road at Volos was a little busy but I was quite happy following cars for a while, in the knowledge that the chance of following someone as stupid as I, was remote and, as such, I would probably not be flying off the side of any more bloody mountains. The main(ish) road seemed to go in the direction my compass recommended so I stuck to it and bumbled along, taking in the sights and sounds.

The decent quality road wiggled its way to the water's edge where I spotted a single fishing boat bobbing up and down. I pulled over and took a photograph, then watched for a while. Having the time to just sit and watch, without feeling the need to push on, was a wonderful thing and completely foreign to my normal life.

I turned inland and made my way into the mountains. As I ascended to the cooler air the traffic thinned considerably and the road began twisting and going back on itself. It was a superb ride and thoroughly enjoyed, the only spoiler being a stonking headache from a lack of coffee.

When I passed a nice-looking café with parking right outside, I pulled in and stopped. As I walked in looking forward to a couple of nice headache-curing coffees, to my amusement I heard my GPS asking me to turn around when possible from inside my tank bag. I smiled at its persistence and ignored it as I found a seat.

'Kalimera,' I said. 'Two double espressos and a bottle of water please.'

'You don't really want a hot drink, do you?'

Nick, the friendly café owner, explained I could

get all the caffeine I needed from a refreshing Freddo espresso. I ordered two, along with a Snickers ice cream and a large bottle of water. I munched down a couple of paracetamol tablets while I waited. Nick told me that he was also a biker and had taught music theory in England a few years back which explained his perfect English. We chatted as I drank my Freddo espressos. They were wonderfully cold, frothy and slipped down a treat.

By the time I reached the villa my headache had almost gone. I rode past and continued to the very end, where there was a wonderful view of the sea and, if you wanted to clamber down, a nice beach. Still feeling a little shaky from my earlier episode, I went no further.

For my return journey, I wanted to take the high road over the mountains. I checked the map, worked out a rough route and followed my nose. Soon I was riding through the village of Kissos, which meant my sense of direction was perfect. Who needs a bloody (minded) GPS eh? I noticed some machinery and slowed to investigate. It turned out it was a ski lift. When you're riding through Greece in 30-something degrees of heat seeing a ski lift comes a bit of a surprise—but I suppose it can snow anywhere if it's high enough.

I made it back without putting a single foot wrong. It helped that there was but one road from Tsagarada to Makrinitsa; the 34, which took me home. The GPS remained in my tank bag and produced muffled complaints all the way. At the hotel I had a shower, then went in search of dinner. I walked up and down for a bit looking at the restaurants, then made a decision and sat down. A waiter handed me the menu and I was over the moon to see rooster with potato. After my rude awakening at God only knows what hour that morning, I thought it most fitting. Unfortunately, the rooster got the last laugh as it was as tough as old boots and not particularly tasty. The restaurant wasn't the kind of place that served Freddo espresso, so I ordered two Greek coffees and read some more of my book.

There were quite a few cats around that looked like they could do with some food but I'd learnt a valuable lesson a few days earlier when I'd dropped a few bits of leftover meat on the ground and found myself in the middle of a bit of a scrap. With this in mind, my leftover rooster stayed on the plate on the table, at least until I was ready to leave.

Every once in a while, I'd look up from my book and see one of the cats edging silently over. Then I noticed something out of the corner of my eye but by the time I looked up, the cat and my leftover rooster, were gone. The cat ran off and disappeared into a hidey-hole to enjoy his well-earned dinner.

A few seconds later a decidedly tired-looking dog plodded past and entered the same little hidey-hole. After a bit of growling and hissing the dog appeared with the rooster. With his head held high, he walked off and disappeared. I couldn't help but feel a little sorry for the cat that had braved the human and won the prize only to have it rudely stolen by a big brute. I joined my hotelier for a scotch and watched as the sun as it disappeared below the horizon.

My route for the day had taken me from Makrinitsa through Ag. Onoufrios, Ano Volos, Agria, Kato Lechonia, Kala Nera, Koropi, Milies, Kalamaki, Lampinou and then to Tsagarada. My return trip took me through Mouresi, Kissos, Chania and Portaria.

Mileage was 75 miles, bringing the total for the trip so far to 3,889 miles.

DAY EIGHTEEN

TUESDAY, 4TH JULY 2017

Sunburnt Leg

HEN I woke at around 7am I felt a bit rubbish; nothing bad, just a lack of energy. I made the decision there and then to have a lazy day.

I read, had breakfast, read some more, had a shower and then wandered around the village looking for sun cream. I didn't find any which was a shame because three hours later I sat down for a relaxing lunch and accidentally cooked my leg until it was red raw. I didn't notice until I stood up to go.

'Bloody hell,' I said, hoping it wasn't as bad as it looked.

As I made my way back to my hotel, I could feel it starting to sting but I told myself it would be fine.

'It's just a bit of sunburn. Man up!'

I had a shower and towel dried my glow-in-the-dark leg, promptly discovering that was not the right thing to do. I placed a cold, wet towel on it for a while which helped, but to stop the pain completely I had to replace the towel every twenty seconds or so. I soon tired of that, got on the bed and just let it hurt. And it did.

The rest of the day was spent trying to read my book and swearing.

DAY NINETEEN

A Lap Of The Pelion

ITH YESTERDAY being a bit of a write-off, I decided to lap the Pelion. My lollipop-red leg certainly looked stupid but didn't hurt that much and surprisingly, I'd managed a half decent night's sleep.

Like all good days, it started with a hearty breakfast. I stuffed my way through two boiled eggs with soldiers, a cheese pastry and a slice of sponge cake, washed down with a couple of sugarless Greek coffees.

When I slipped into my heavyweight leather trousers, the leg screamed merry hell. By the time I got to my bike it was stinging like a bastard and I was keen to get underway but—shock horror—there was a problem.

My bike had been moved from near the front of the parking place to the very back and was completely blocked in by cars. I looked for a way to get it out but there was absolutely no way I was going anywhere.

I should explain here that there are actually two Richard Georgious. There's the calm one who's patient, reasonably emotionally intelligent and a bit of a thinker. The calm one hates making a scene. Then there's the angry one who has zero patience, zero tolerance and doesn't give a damn about making a scene, in fact, the messier the better. Cross the angry one at your peril. Both are completely necessary but don't care much for each other. The calm one is very nervous of the angry one but understands that he is sometimes necessary. The angry one detests the calm one and thinks he's a wimp.

As I stood there looking at my bike stuck in the corner, I felt myself move slightly towards Mr Angry, but Mr Calm was still in control. I walked over to some of the gift shops nearby to enquire if anyone knew who owned the cars blocking me in, but they were closed. This pushed me one step closer to Mr Angry. I took a walk into the square and politely asked there. Nope. Another step closer.

The church was empty, so I visited a nearby restaurant. I could feel the power starting to surge through my body as they told me they couldn't help. Mr Calm was struggling to stay in control. I went back to my bike and checked again for an escape route but found nothing. I checked the cars to see if any of them were unlocked so I could take off the handbrake and push them but no luck. It was at this point that Mr Calm got overruled. Mr Angry came storming in.

'Fucking hell!'

Mr Angry mounted the bike and started it up, revving it get attention. He then placed his thumb on the horn and left it there. This caused quite a stir. People came from all directions and, when enough people had arrived, he removed his thumb from the horn.

'These cars have blocked me in, and I need some help moving them,' he said, loudly.

With Mr Angry oozing confidence and ability, it wasn't long before the place was a flurry of activity. One man came literally running over with some keys and moved the car in front of my bike. Mr Angry accepted his apology with a slight nod and rode off towards the Pelion.

While Mr Angry was in control everything felt fine but as Mr Calm started to return, guilt appeared on the horizon. Five miles later I was full of regrets. What a scene, oh the humiliation, my bike will get vandalised, everyone will hate me…

'Everyone hates you already!' said the fading remnants of Mr Angry.

I was unhappy but it was in the past and it had served its purpose—I was on the road. My aim was simply to see the Pelion, especially the southernmost part, and what better way to do that than to ride its length to the end. I didn't really fancy the area surrounding Volos as it would be full of traffic, so I started with a trip over the mountains to Kissos.

After my lengthy departure, my sunburnt leg wasn't happy either and riding along with the sun blasting down on my black leather trousers wasn't helping. Just after Chania, as I began climbing up the mountain the air cooled, and a layer of cloud blocked much of the sun's heat which was very welcome. The mountain topped out at about 3,500ft and with the clouds zooming past just above my head, I pulled over as my leg cooled a little.

A few miles after Kissos, I noticed the name of the road change from the wonderfully simple 34 to Epar.Od.Agiou. Dimitriou-Agiou.Ioanni. Just rolls off the tongue that, doesn't it? The ride to the south of the Pelion was superb. The mountain roads twisted and turned back on themselves and there was always something to look at. The only problem I had was the burning from my leg. The day warmed up and my leg grew hotter and hotter. Ignoring it was easy at first, what with the amazing scenery, but it wasn't long before the balance between pleasure and pain changed. There not being a damned thing I could do about it, I accepted it was going to hurt and continued onwards.

By the time I'd reached Chorto I'd realised there was a limit to how long one can appreciate beautiful scenery. The Pelion continuously spoiled me with views of the western or eastern coastline, and the unrelenting beauty soon became passé.

When I saw a delightful little harbour set back from the water, I pulled in. While clambering off my bike I noticed a café; perfect. As I pulled up a seat at a table right on the water's edge, the couple on the next table glanced over.

I did my best to place an order with the elderly lady for

a double Greek coffee without sugar but got into a right pickle. She rabbited away in Greek and I waited patiently for a pause.

'You know, I haven't got a clue what you're saying.' I said.

I did the polite thing and waited for her to finish. But she didn't. Instead she continued, and she continued some more. I raised my hands, hoping she understood the generic 'I surrender' signal but even that didn't stop her. The couple on the next table shrugged.

'Can't help,' said the lady, 'we got the same.'

I held out a 20 Euro note in the hope this would aid the situation. My money was promptly taken and the lady gestured for me to follow to the kitchen. She gave me a coffee and a cake, then disappeared through a door.

It turned out the couple were from Kent, so we chatted about this and that. I hope I didn't overdo it; I can talk for England sometimes.

Eventually the elderly lady returned with the tray from her till. I realised the problem — she didn't have enough change for the note. She gestured for me to return to her kitchen and pointed to the things she had. I had another cake and stocked up on water, lots of water.

After saying goodbye to the couple, I loaded the water onto my bike and departed. As I meandered around the wonderful roads, I marvelled at the machine that got me there. My motorcycle seemed to have come into its own since its terrifying flight down the hillside. The sound from its engine was pure mechanical perfection and its exhaust seemed a little raspier than before. It was a true pleasure to ride.

That said, my body was not so enamoured. My arse was killing me, my leg was on fire, my right knee wanted to be straight and my left calf was cramping. I got off and walked around for a bit. I noticed a rather worrying rumble in my stomach and hoped I'd make it back to my hotel before it got any worse.

The ride through the southern part of the Pelion really was incredibly pretty. The combination of the wiggly coastline, blue-green waters, the weather and winding roads made it a truly unforgettable experience. Looking at photographs of the area show how beautiful the place is, but it was more than that. I was feeling the freedom of being on an adventure on my motorbike, and this made it infinitely more special. Unfortunately, I was also feeling lots of activity in my stomach that wasn't so wonderful.

When I reached the village at the end of the Pelion I was half blown away by the scenery and half terrified of being caught short. Out of Trikeri, the road ended and that was the end of the Pelion—I'd made it. I turned the bike around, looked at my watch and worked out some rough times. It had taken me about four hours. Feeling more activity from my stomach, I was aware that also meant it was going to take me four hours to ride back.

'Please don't let anything bad happen.'

As I rode back, it became apparent I was going to need to stop somewhere. I couldn't remember passing any cafes or restaurants for quite some time which meant I only had one option—and that filled me with fear. Happily, in my life thus far, not once had I ever been forced to poop in the woods, but it looked like that was about to change, and I wasn't pleased.

I felt incredibly uncomfortable. Just as I could hold on no more I went around a bend and was confronted by the perfect place to stop—lots of trees and a bank. I pulled in, unzipped my 'in case of emergency' pocket in my tank bag and removed two packets of tissues.

'I can't believe I'm doing this. Bloody hell Richard.'

The cramps in my stomach made it crystal clear there was no time to secure the bike. I hastily went down the steep bank and found a spot. Not having ever pooped in the woods before I didn't know the procedures. I removed my trousers and boxers and dug a reasonably sized hole with my hands in the soft ground, hoping I was the first to use that particular spot.

As I crouched in the most unflattering of positions, I felt on the verge of panic and expected to see a farmer or a family out on a pre-picnic walk. Thankfully I remained completely alone throughout the entire experience. With everything completed, buried and covered up nicely, I made my way back to the bike. Feeling a huge sense of relief, I popped the remaining tissues back into the pocket and rode off happy in the knowledge that I was no longer a 'poop in the woods' virgin. Given enough practice, perhaps next time I'm caught short I might even be able to keep my trousers on.

The ride was unhurried and as beautiful as any other. My mind started ticking and the next thing I knew I was comparing the feelings I get while leaving a ferry with those experienced while having a poo in the woods. I decided I'm a complicated creature and that I need to do a world trip to reach some kind of conclusion on that.

By the time I got back to Makrinitsa most of the day had gone. I parked my bike where it was unlikely to get blocked in. As I lugged my stuff through the village, I surreptitiously checked if anyone recognised me from my earlier episode. There seemed to be a little bit of pointing and whispering going on, but that could well have been paranoia. On the bright side, I didn't have to worry about being blocked in again.

I half expected the hotel owner to mention my outburst but there was nothing. I just about managed to drag my stuff up to my room before stripping off and collapsing on the bed. It would have been so easy to have closed my eyes and allowed myself to drift off, but I had the beginnings of a headache from lack of caffeine, so going out for a coffee was mandatory.

I showered, then ambled through the village, guided by just my nose. The third restaurant I passed won me over with the most delightful aroma. I told the waitress I'd have what I could smell. It turned out to be pan-fried chicken and it was just as delicious as the one I'd had before. For dessert, they only had chocolate cake left. I chose the chocolate cake.

'Are you trying to kill me?' I asked, as she placed it on the table.

Dribbled over the top of the cake was a thick layer of melted badness that screamed heart-attack. She smiled back in one of those 'polite but just shut up you boring old fart' kind of ways and left. It tasted divine. I didn't attempt any small talk when the waitress appeared with a jug of coffee. Instead I smiled in a 'you don't know anything you silly little youngster' way and continued reading my book. Happy with my fix of caffeine I wandered back to the hotel and went to bed.

The route for today was Makrinitsa, Portaria, Chania, Kissos, Mouresi, Tsagkarada, Xorychti, Lampinou, Neochori, Chorto, Milina and Trikeri. Then pretty much the same for the return journey.

Mileage was 147 miles, bringing the total for the trip so far to 4,036 miles.

DAY TWENTY

A Walk Through Portaria

THE HOTEL owner had told me about a very scenic walk in the neighbouring village so with a day to spare before meeting up with my loveliness, there was no better time. I had breakfast, making sure I had lots of strong coffee, and set off towards Portaria.

With the village only about two miles away and the day being young, the walk was easy and pleasant. The sun was not yet in full swing and although there wasn't a single cloud in the sky, the air hadn't had time enough to warm up much above 25 degrees. I ambled along absorbing the view, and as is often the case, I saw so much more because I was walking.

After about a mile I passed a rather nondescript building where something was definitely going on. Going by the grunts, groans and the sound of balls being whacked against a wall it had to be a squash hall. I thought about playing squash in this temperature and shook my head. I hope it was air-conditioned.

When I reached the shaded archway that marked the beginning of the route, I drank from the fountain. The shade from the huge tree just outside the entrance provided a welcome change.

Beyond the archway and in the woods, the light almost disappeared making my cool, green surroundings feel like a secret new world. A stream meandered its way through the undergrowth and small columns of light illuminated the woodland floor. The sound of running water is always a pleasure but after the walk from Makrinitsa, it was even more welcome. I removed my camera lens cap, composed and fired. The resulting photograph was okay but could not really be compared to the open, three-dimensional world in front of me.

The route climbed through tiny overhung pathways, rickety wooden bridges and over boulders worn by the feet of walkers for what looked like hundreds of years. My choice of footwear, the humble flip-flop, made some of the sections a little testing. More than once I found myself slip-sliding on a rock, but I never actually fell over.

I took lots of photographs, being careful to check the exposure and compensating when necessary, but none of them really did the place justice. It's one of those places that needs to be appreciated in the flesh. The two-dimensional single plane of a photograph is not enough to even begin to show the place in all its glory.

After about an hour or so I could feel my legs beginning to shake. I surprised to see how far I'd come and how high I'd climbed. A few minutes later I reached the end of the walk and sat on some very photogenic stairs to chill a while.

Then I exited the woods back out into the heat and direct sunlight. The change from dark and green to bright and brown was a rude shock to the system, and it took my eyes a while to adjust. I foolishly assumed I knew where I was and decided to walk via the road instead of through the woods.

After about an hour, I was surprised that I didn't recognise the road at all. I assumed this was because I was on the part that skipped back to the beginning of the walk. After a further hour or so of walking, I still didn't recognise anything which was a little worrying. When I eventually came across someone, I asked.

'Makrinitsa?'

She pointed in the direction of where I'd come. The look on my face must have told the complete story as she laughed and offered her bottle of water. She then pointed to my flip-flops and laughed some more. In her eyes, I could see the word 'idiot'. I thanked her and turned down the water, about turned and allowed my wobbly legs to carry me home.

The walk back seemed to take forever. I started doubting the direction I was going in but continued anyway. After what felt like an eternity, I reached Portaria and the beginning of the wooded walk. At this point, I knew where I was and that I had two miles left to go. I had a good long drink from the fountain by the archway and Plodded my way back to Makrinitsa. Walking in temperatures of about 40 degrees is not much fun and by the time I got back I was knackered and looking forward to getting off my feet. Flip-flops are great sometimes, and other times they're not so great.

My four or five-mile walk ended up being more like ten miles which, in intense heat, was bloody hard work. After a shower and a nap, I ventured out for my evening meal. As I waited for a fillet of chicken to arrive, I thought about meeting up with my wife and friends. My mind zipped back to 2009 and I found myself immersed in the memories of when I'd met up with them in Ibiza on my way back from the Sahara.

I'd had a hard time in Morocco and was looking forward to a break (as well as seeing my loveliness and friends, obviously). As I rode into the campsite, I'd spotted my welcoming committee. Everyone was there, cheering and smiling. It was a wonderful moment and I remembered it fondly. I was secretly hoping for another memorable welcome.

After food and coffee, I peeled my thighs off the rock-hard wooden chair. Makrinitsa had been a good host and I was going to miss its slow pace and tranquillity.

DAY TWENTY-ONE

Mr Angry And The GPS

BEING THE kind of person who is never late, I awoke to the pressure of a deadline. I was due to meet my wife and friends at 2pm, which gave me seven hours—an ample amount of time. But even just having a deadline meant the pressure was on. I showered and indulged in some scrambled egg, toast, sponge cake and coffee.

I checked Facebook and found that my friends Carl and Frances, who were travelling Europe in a giant camper van called Blossom, were in Kato Gatzea. It would have been completely out of the question not to pay them a visit, so I adjusted my route and smiled at the thought of seeing them.

I paid up, packed up and dressed up, then lugged everything back to the bike—in exactly the same place where I'd left it, with no one parked in front. In fact, it looked like everyone had given it a wide berth.

'I wonder why that is,' I said, grinning.

It was set to be another scorcher and as much as I hated the idea of being stuck in traffic in the heat, I needed a cash machine and the best place to find one was Volos. Paying the hotel bill had completely cleaned me out of cash, which meant no café stops. Out of the question! Plus, I'd need money for the coming days.

Before setting off I checked my phone for messages from Flowie but there were none. I sent her a message: 'Wif, still on target for two, how exciting! Husb x'

A couple of miles before reaching Volos, I asked the GPS to find a cash machine. The next 20 minutes were spent battling the heat and stop-start traffic but eventually I arrived, except there was no cash machine. I picked the next one on the list but again, no bloody machine.

The combination of the heat, traffic, a deadline and not being able to find a machine was starting to piss me off. Mr Angry was edging his way in.

'Do you want to fucking help or not?' I shouted angrily at the GPS.

I picked a third cash machine and when it drew another blank, Mr Angry was waiting. I removed the GPS from my handlebar, threw it on the ground and jumped up and down on it like a spoilt three-year-old having a paddy.

'Fucking wanking thing!' I hollered.

When I'd finished, I calmly picked it up and stuffed it into my tank bag.

'You have arrived at your destination.'

'Fuck off!'

I removed my helmet and jacket and leant against the bike. That's when I noticed I had a small audience. I smiled and apologised the best I could, but no one said anything. Instead they just stared with concerned expressions. This was an opportunity.

I removed my bank card from my wallet and pretended to insert it into a cash machine. I then typed my pin number into the imaginary keypad while making beep-boop-beep-beep noises. I could see everyone relax and a few smiles broke through.

'Cash machine?' I asked.

A big chap standing by my side took me through some alleyways and up the road, and after a few minutes we arrived at a cash machine. I withdrew my cash and handed the chap five Euro note. He thanked me but didn't take it. Instead he told me to be happy. Sometimes it was difficult, but I decided to try harder in future.

When I arrived back at my bike most of the crowd was still there, which was lucky because my keys were in the ignition and my tank bag containing important stuff was wide open. It was a surreal moment; everyone seemed excited that I'd managed to withdraw money. There was lots of laughter, handshaking and conversing in Greek. One lady even stood next to me and took a selfie with her phone. I thanked everyone once more and, feeling a little confused, got the hell out of Volos.

The traffic thinned and the moving air made the heat a bit less oppressive. I was happily zipping along, wondering if my earlier audience had mistaken me for someone famous or important when I spotted a shop full to the brim with stuff. Thinking it might sell sun cream, I pulled over and had a nose. They did; it was 17 Euros for a tiny bottle that looked like it contained just enough for one helping. I decided I'd rather be burnt to death than spend 17 Euros on that and rode off.

When I reached the campsite where Carl and Frances were staying, I rode in and parked next to Blossom, their camper van. Time was ticking on so I sent another message to my wife: 'Wif, with Carl and Frances, might be a little late. Husb x'

There were no messages from my loveliness, so I assumed everything was on schedule at her end and went to the beach to meet my friends. When they saw my annoying little face, it was laughs and smiles all around. I stripped off my leathers, grabbed a small beer and we bobbed around in the sea drinking and chatting. It was wonderful. I'd spent almost three weeks away from everyone I knew and seeing familiar faces felt good.

We went back to Blossom, took some photographs and arranged to meet up properly in the coming days. I rode off excited about seeing Flowie and welcoming committee.

I could feel the excitement building as I rode the last hundred yards to the villa. When I finally arrived outside, there was nothing. I tried calling but my phone just beeped and switched off. I walked up the driveway wondering which door to try first when one of them opened and my wonderful wife appeared in the doorway.

'I thought you were dead you fucking bastard!' she said, bursting into tears.

Then she thumped me.

It turned out my phone had not been working for the last few days and all the messages I'd sent her, and the messages she's sent me, hadn't worked. She'd also tried calling but that wasn't working either. Unfortunately, she'd taken my silence to mean I'd crashed. She was incredibly unhappy, and I was incredibly in the shit.

And, on top of all that, she'd had a bit of a ding-dong with one of our friends and there was no way she was going to stay in the same place as 'that arsehole' so we had to find some new accommodation and another hire car. She'd not slept for 48 hours and hadn't eaten all day. This was not the welcome I was hoping for.

We set off in the borrowed hire car to find another place to stay. After drawing a few blanks, the tension became so high that one more could well have resulted in my murder. Luckily, an apartment on the side of a hill with a fantastic view over the sea was soon secured for the night and a little while after that, we drove around looking for our friends. After unsuccessfully going from one place to another for about an hour we gave up and found a restaurant.

Flowie did her best to make polite conversation, but she was exhausted and just wanted to sleep. We enjoyed/

endured a short evening and made our way back to our room.

The route for today was Makrinitsa, Volos, Kato Gatzea, Tsagkarada.

Mileage was a rather modest 66 miles, bringing the total for the trip so far to 4,102 miles.

DAY TWENTY-TWO

SATURDAY, 8TH JULY 2017

Hand Gestures

NOISY AIR conditioning and uncomfortable bed ruined any chances of a good sleep and we both woke feeling fragile and grumpy. On top of that, the day ahead was full of horrible logistics like finding somewhere else to stay for the week and sorting out the hire cars.

Our plan for the day was breakfast, accommodation, hire cars, motorbike, relax.

If Flowie didn't eat breakfast within an hour or so of getting up, she'd start to feel grumpy and sick so that was our first priority. We didn't hang around—everything was packed and after paying our bill, we set off to hunt down our first meal of the day. It didn't go well.

I'm about as non-fussy as it gets and will eat just about anything at any time. Flowie is a little more particular. This made getting breakfast a bit trickier than I was used to. After a number of failed stops, we settled for a bakery, but they were pretty much sold out, so I purchased some almost fresh croissants. As I bit into one end, a surprisingly large dollop of custard fell out of the other. This landed on the groin of my shorts then promptly slid down onto the seat of the hire car. I glanced at Flowie as I scooped up the clot of custard from between my legs, hoping she hadn't noticed but her face told me otherwise. Credit where credit's due, she didn't say a word.

When we arrived in Agios Ioannis we found a hotel next to the beach and booked up for the week. Accommodation secured, it was time to sort out the hire car situation. The car we had needed to be given back to our friends, but we needed it to get to a car hire place to hire one of our own. Once there, Flowie would then drive our friend's car back to their place and I'd follow. Flowie would then drive our car back to the hotel and I'd follow on my motorbike. If it all went according to plan, we'd have it done by the evening and be able to relax.

In the ideal world, we'd have had a car delivered direct to the hotel but in the real world, this was not possible. Our friendly hotel receptionist found us the next best option; a car hire company in Volos. Unfortunately, the directions were a little vague at best, and completely unfathomable at worst. I cringed as the receptionist explained the one-way system to Flowie.

'You're supposed to keep to the left and do a lap of the block, then turn right just before the road where you got on. Most people though, just turn right immediately and go the wrong way through the lights.'

My brain can't cope but Flowie is excellent at things like that. She wrote it down and we set off. I decided to take my GPS just in case.

It all went perfectly until we got within a mile of the place. We went the right way around the one-way system, the wrong way around the one-way system, drove up and down just about every road in the vicinity but, for the life of us, we just couldn't find it. In the end, we parked up and walked.

Unbeknown to us, the reason we couldn't find it was because the name of the company was different to the name of the sign on their shop. Needless to say, by the time we found the bloody place tensions were running high.

A car was duly hired and when the time came to pay up, we were told: 'Our card machine is broken. We only accept cash.'

Not only that, the price had gone up considerably from what we were told over the phone and the car was not far off from being an old banger. Not wanting to fuck up an already fucked up day any further, we accepted the car and paid a large lump of cash.

Flowie was confident she knew the way to our friend's place in Tsagkarada but in case she made a mistake, she asked me to follow using the GPS. All was fine for the first five minutes, then she veered off course. I overtook and used the GPS to get us out of Volos and back on track.

But the GPS started playing around and the next thing I knew I'd turned off the road onto a tiny track. Flowie came to my rescue, beeping her horn as she overtook. She waved her arm out the window and gestured vigorously, indicating her frustration. I returned to the main road and followed.

When we eventually arrived, our friends weren't there but that didn't matter—we had arrived. Flowie parked their car in the driveway and wrote a note while I changed into my motorcycle clobber.

When I'd dressed earlier, it was so hot and humid I'd decided to skip my boxer shorts and wear just my shorts instead. My bike was parked on the road, so I checked I had the all-clear before taking them off. It was a weird feeling, standing there completely naked from the waist down. I was getting ready to hoick my left leg into my trousers when I spotted a couple walking towards me. If they weren't there, I would have been able to keep my balance and slip into my leathers easily; however, with the added urgency I lost my balance and ended hopping around like an idiot. My little white bum bouncing around as I struggled must have been a horrid sight. I'm not sure if they noticed me but nothing was said as they walked by.

With my bottom safely cocooned in my leather trousers and a note left for our friends, we departed Tsagkarada and headed to our hotel. The time since meeting up had been quite tough, especially for Flowie, and I was looking forward to enjoying a nice evening with my lovely lady.

My brain was already sitting at the beachside bar drinking, laughing and eating.

We chilled for a bit, put on fresh clothes and made our way outside. We walked along the main drag until we found the perfect place to spend the evening. We ordered, drank, laughed, drank, ate and drank, then we drank some more. It was wonderful sharing the evening with my wife. With all the chores of the day complete we were finally able to let our hair down.

I picked a delicious-sounding dish from the menu; basically, lamb cutlets with potatoes and vegetables in a nice herby sauce. The first thing I noticed when it arrived was the colour. It was grey and looked like no lamb I'd ever seen before. I ate the tasteless lump anyway and was amused to notice that it had exactly the same texture as a rubber He-Man action figure I used to chew on as a child.

Being wine people, the copious volumes of ouzos soon caught up with us and the conversation changed to things like 'I think it might be time to go home' and 'can you remember where we live' and even 'I think I might sleep in the bathroom tonight.'

Our alcohol-induced zig-zagging meant the 300-yard trip to the hotel took ages but we must have eventually got back because we woke up in our own bed.

The mileage for the day was six miles, bringing the total for the trip so far to 4,108 miles.

ONE MAN ON A BIKE

DAY TWENTY-THREE

SUNDAY, 9TH JULY 2017

A Lazy Sunday

SUNDAY WAS spent exactly how Sundays are supposed to be, lounging around doing nothing. We swam a little, ate a little, bathed in the sun a little then swam a little more. At around midday, we stumbled across our friends and decided to do lunch together. Everyone chatted, laughed and joked and it seemed like the terse words at the beginning of the holiday were firmly relegated to history.

I looked over the menu. What I really wanted was the lamb but after the previous day's experience, it was best avoided. I chose spaghetti bolognaise, thinking I was playing it safe, but it had a quarter inch of liquid in the bottom and no taste whatsoever. I ate it nonetheless but complained that it wasn't good when we paid. It was good to be with our friends once again.

After a much-needed afternoon nap, Flowie and I went

out for some gentle evening drinks. We found a place on the beach, bought a couple of Metaxas and enjoyed watching the sun slip below the horizon. When I asked for the bill, I was a little surprised to see that two Metaxas and two coffees cost just over 40 Euros. I'm bloody glad we didn't go for a full on piss up!

DAY TWENTY-FOUR

Mamma Mia

MONDAY BEGAN exactly how all Mondays should—with a hearty full English breakfast and a lounge on the beach. Would the world not be a better place?

Next on the list was Damouchari. This was the beach where one of the scenes from Mamma Mia was filmed and as luck would have it, was just a walk away from where we were staying.

Over the next hour, we discovered that the walk was more of a hike and a bloody arduous one at that. First it took us up a long, steep slope, then up a number of huge steps which seemed to take us all over the place—including through people's gardens. Once that had been navigated, it took us out onto a piece of road so steep I kept slipping out of my flip-flops and could only get up it by walking backward. Luckily that was the end of the ascent.

We found a tree with a taxi driver's business card nailed to it, perfectly placed. I noted it down just in case.

After a few hundred yards of walking along a reasonably flat road, it was time for the descent, which was just as arduous. By the time we arrived at Damouchari we were completely knackered and ready for a drink. We found a restaurant, picked a place and sat down.

The little cove where the scene was filmed was beautiful, but it hadn't really been looked after and didn't have the magic I was expecting. The wooden platform that the cast of the movie danced on before jumping off was gone but the place was still reasonably recognisable. We ordered some drinks and talked for a while as our bodies recovered.

As we made our way back from Damouchari we noticed a girl, dressed in a very small bikini, posing on a rock jutting out from the sea. A drone circled around her taking photographs. She pouted, stuck out her bottom, changed sides, smiled, did girly waves, poked out her boobs, ponced around with her hair, stuck out her tongue, dazzled the world with her whiter-than-white teeth, poured water down her cleavage and lots more besides. This was a woman who took selfies into an entirely new dimension.

Personally, I struggle taking selfies. I aim my finger over the button, carefully turn the phone around, then try to press the button from behind. Unfortunately, by the time I've turned my phone around, stuck out my arse, pouted and told myself I'm a tart, my finger has moved, and nothing happens. I then move my finger around guessing where the button is and eventually get a selfie. It's a system that does produce one, however, the high levels of concentration involved usually result in me looking like I'm desperate for a shit. Perhaps I too need a gyroscopically controlled, artificially intelligent, flying camera.

Just before we reached our hotel, we passed the campsite where Carl and Frances were staying and popped in to say hello. I amazed everyone by showing off a new grammar rule Flowie taught me — that a verb is a 'doing' word — and we arranged to join up for our evening meal.

After a brief nap and a shower, it was back out onto the main drag for dinner as planned. The evening went well, we laughed, drank, ate and told stories until dark, then continued for another couple of hours until they turned the light off and started putting the tables away. Hint taken.

DAY TWENTY-FIVE

TUESDAY, 11TH JULY 2017

Little To Report

TUESDAY STARTED exactly how all Tuesdays should—with another hearty full English. The sensible part of me worried ever so slightly about things like heart attacks and obesity but was quickly overruled by the other 99 per cent.

We booked a boat for the following day, had an afternoon nap, read our books and lounged on the beach and before we knew it the best part of the day was upon us; the evening.

We met up with our friends for dinner and found a nice restaurant by the beach. After questioning our waiter at length, I stupidly ordered the lamb. It turned out to be goat but not wanting to make a scene I ate it anyway and it was okay. Flowie ordered prawns and shrimps which doubled the bill, but we all enjoyed our evening and lived to tell the tale.

ONE MAN ON A BIKE

DAY TWENTY-SIX

WEDNESDAY, 12TH JULY 2017

A Day On The Aegean

THERE'S NOTHING quite like feeling the sun's rays on your face as you power your way through the Aegean in a small boat.

We arrived at the booking office 15 minutes early. It was all smiles and excitement at that point. Ten minutes went by, then 20, then half an hour. We went outside to get some fresh air, waited another half an hour and then asked where our boat was.

'It's coming,' said the lady.

An hour later it eventually arrived. We got our boat at eleven—two hours late.

After being stuck in a hot office for more than two hours and stressing, being out on the open water was an absolute pleasure. Flowie had a smile from ear to ear which was wonderful to see, and I thoroughly enjoyed being captain of the ship.

Our first stop was to pick up Carl and Frances who were about fifteen minutes away. I drove the boat right up to the beach and allowed our guests to get on. The rope ladder was all but useless. With legs and arses poking out in all sorts of directions they finally managed it. We departed the beach and headed south.

Our little boat may have been a bit of a banger but when the throttle was pushed forward it had a surprising turn of speed. When the lever was pulled back the bloody thing stopped so quickly that everyone shot forward and almost fell off, which proved to be most entertaining.

We visited a number of beaches and everything was great but for one exception; getting back on to the bloody thing was all but impossible. Flowie just about managed to clamber aboard and in doing so cut her arm. Carl then showed her how to do it properly and cut his arm in exactly the same place, which made us all laugh a lot. Poor Carl.

By early afternoon we'd found an almost deserted little beach with an open taverna. We enjoyed a good lunch and some not too shoddy wine. The food was fantastic and just what was needed. After a small swim and a doze, we explored more places. The day ticked on and it was soon time to head back.

After dropping off our friends we chugged back to the harbour to hand the boat back. When we arrived, the man who'd given us the boat was unhappy. Apparently, we were very late, and they were about to call the harbour people and send out a search team. We explained how we'd collected the boat two hours late and that we were only one hour late in dropping it off, so we were actually early. Unfortunately, that didn't wash at all and we got a bit of a bollocking.

From there we had to go back to the boat hire office to get our receipt. When the lady asked why we were so late, Flowie calmly explained the ins and outs of customer service and the difference between right and wrong. That didn't go down particularly well and there was a bit of an argument. Needless to say, we won't be returning to 'those arseholes' again when we need a boat in the future.

We enjoyed a quiet evening and good food and retired early after what felt like an exhausting day.

ONE MAN ON A BIKE

DAY TWENTY-SEVEN

Sardines And Another Steep Track

FLOWIE AND I discussed our plans for the day over the mandatory full English. First, we'd meet up with Sue, Nick, Linda and Denis, the friends Flowie flew out with. Then we'd jump into two cars and go to Elephant Beach, a scenic beach reasonably close by. We'd seen photographs and it looked very nice.

'Christ almighty.'

I got my first view of it as we climbed down the steep steps. It was absolutely heaving. Now, I like people almost as much as the next person but I'm a little bit funny in that I don't like to smell them or see their wobbly bits up close. With everyone else talking about how beautiful it was I decided to keep my mouth firmly closed. It was but one day and who was I to spoil it?

We looked around for a square inch to call home for the next few hours, squeezing around people and apologising before laying our towels down and poking our sun brolly into the ground.

The gentle breeze brought forth the aroma of sweaty crevices and coconut sun cream. My natural instinct was to go back to the car but that would have been unfair on the others, so I went for a swim. I managed to get to the sea without treading on anyone and bobbed up and down in the warm water.

A small wave pushed me backward and I bumped into a chap. He looked at me and shuddered, then shook his head like after you have a wee. When I felt the temperature of the water change, I put two and two together and briskly swam away, keeping my mouth closed. I decided it was time to go back to re-join the others. I found a path through a concentrated line of bodies and carefully sat on my piece of towel trying, unsuccessfully, to keep it from sinking into the sand. I gave up, folded it into a pillow and laid down with my book.

With the beach being so packed, I understood the need for people to step over me so I did my best to remain calm. But when a drop of sweat from a fat woman's arse landed on my lip, I'd had enough.

'That's it!' I exclaimed, 'I can't stay here a moment longer.'

I picked up my towel. Flowie and our friends did the same and no one looked upset. As we made our way back to the cars Flowie suggested we return to where we'd visited yesterday when we'd had the boat. Not only was it pretty much deserted, it also had a taverna which served great food and wine.

We had just a small map and Flowie's built-in compass to guide us. I was completely useless as I had absolutely no idea where we were or where we were going but I nodded when it felt right to nod and agreed with everything Flowie said.

We headed down a small track, scuffing the bottom of our cars. When the road deteriorated further, we evened up the load by moving Denis to our car. The road got smaller, steeper and bumpier and then it pretty much disappeared altogether. Being hardened adventurers, we continued anyway. With only a few hundred yards to go, we came across another car coming the other way. This was a problem.

The poor Audi driver and his girlfriend had been trying unsuccessfully to get up the very steep track for the last half an hour. When they finally made it, they found we'd blocked their path completely and had to stop. Oops!

We introduced ourselves and examined the situation for solutions. The best we could come up with was for me to drive out to the very edge of the track and see if they could squeeze past. This I did but when the ground moved slightly, I decided it was a terrible idea and stopped. Landing upside down on the beach from a height of about 50ft wasn't my idea of fun so the Romanian couple had no choice but to reverse the Audi down onto the beach so we could pass. They also helped us to get our cars safely onto the beach before attempting their ascent once more. What a lovely couple.

We parked up and had a nervous laugh about it. I'm quite sure the trip back up was in our minds but it wasn't mentioned once.

We swam, lounged in our own space, stretched out, climbed on the rocks, read books and relaxed. We then descended on the taverna and enjoyed a well-earned lunch with copious amounts of food and wine.

Nick and I discussed various methods of getting our plucky little cars up the steep track while the others taunted us with their glasses of wine. After seeing the Audi having such a difficult time, we were concerned but with both stupidity and persistence on our side, we were confident we'd make it up one way or another.

The problem we had to overcome was that our cars had almost no power so if we went slowly, the engine would just stall. If we revved the engine and used the clutch to stay slow, we'd probably burn it out. This meant we had one option—hit the slope at speed.

We needn't have worried. Other than a few expensive-sounding crunching noises, our cars bounced their way up the track admirably. When we reached the top, I gave Denis back and we returned to our respective homes. Our trip down the track to the beach left me feeling that we'd had a day of adventure rather than a day on holiday. It also left me feeling excited about getting back on the bike and riding through Greece to Igoumenitsa.

We had a nap and went out to eat. We discussed the following day which was to be comprised of Flowie driving to Volos and me following on the bike. We'd then say our goodbyes and depart separately. Flowie would get a lift to the airport and I'd ride through Greece to Igoumenitsa to catch the ferry to Brindisi in Italy.

Originally, Flowie was going to be spending another week in Greece but given that she wasn't staying with our friends, she'd decided to leave when I did. This meant that not only was her holiday twice the price, it was half the length. This combined with the fact we were parting made the evening feel sad and I wasn't looking forward to saying goodbye the following day.

DAY TWENTY-EIGHT

FRIDAY, 14TH JULY 2017

Departure And Sadness

WE ATE breakfast as normal but as is often the case on last days, there was sadness in the air. Not only were we going home, we were going home separately and on top of that I felt bad for Flowie as her holiday hadn't been great.

We got lost on the way to Volos but arrived at the car hire place in good time. After promising to keep a close eye on my mobile phone for messages and making sure everything was okay with Flowie and the car, I kissed her goodbye and rode off into the Volos traffic.

It felt horrible but I wasn't going to get home by moping around and if I could muster up some enthusiasm, there was still some fun to have. Riding the breadth of Greece, catching the ferry to Italy and riding up through Italy and then France wasn't your normal boring ride home, and I hoped the feeling of adventure would return in force.

Out of Volos, I examined the map. It was a pretty straightforward ride to Igoumenitsa. First, I'd first aim for Larissa on the E92 and E75, I'd then skirt Larissa and continue onwards on the E92. At Panagia, I'd switch to the 2, which would take me all the way to Igoumenitsa.

As I plotted the route into my GPS, I thought about how easy it would be to follow the magenta line and not take in the places I passed through. It may well have been the tail-end of my adventure, but it was still quite a ride in itself. Even though I would be taking the fast roads, I'd try my very best to take in as much as possible.

I enjoyed the ride as much as I could, but the heat made it uncomfortable. I stopped at a petrol station, filled up with premium unleaded, filled the Thermos with fresh coffee and filled the empty spaces in my panniers with food and goodies. I tied my jacket to the back of the bike and stood in my T-shirt, listening to the two halves of my brain arguing.

'All the gear all the time,' said my sensible side.

My sensible side is incredibly small and was immediately overruled by my fun side. And with that, I jumped on the bike and rode off towards Igoumenitsa in my T-shirt. I rode carefully and kept my speed down but there was no getting around the fact I was going to be very early. I'd have a fair amount of time to kill before my 11pm sailing. When I eventually arrived at the port, it was two—I was nine hours early.

'That's a lot of cake and coffee.'

Time went incredibly slowly. I would never have believed it but there's only so much cake and coffee one man can eat. I rode around the area a few times and found different places to eat cake and drink coffee but however you juggle it, nine hours is a long time.

At six, I checked in and sat in the port building reading. I was engrossed in the story when I heard a kind of weird buzzing. A man was being shaken senseless in the most violent massage chair I've ever seen. He was holding his phone out in front of him and was almost shouting 'Get this baby!' I tried to give him five as I walked by, but the chair was shaking him around so much I doubt whether he even saw me.

I read some more, bought some Greece stickers for my bike and had another coffee. When we were finally told to queue for boarding, I rode up to the front and stopped next to a biker couple. They were lovely. We swapped stories in the weird orange light of the dock until we were allowed to board.

Inside, I almost had the ferry to myself. There were two large rooms, one at the front and one at the back. I had the one at the front all to myself and made the most of it. I grabbed a bite to eat, then made a very comfortable bed out of cushions and slept like a baby for the next eight hours.

My route for the day was Agios Ioannis, Volos, Larissa, Trikala, Kalabaka, Malakasi, Pedini and finally Igoumenitsa.

Mileage was 230 miles, bringing the total for the trip so far to 4,338 miles.

DAY TWENTY-NINE

Determined To Like Italy

J UNE AND July are usually excellent months for my little business with lots of sales but with me being away and unable to tinker in my normal ways, sales had taken a big hit. As such, I was keen to get back so I could attempt to find out what was going on and try to fix it. This was a shame as I was looking forward to meandering my way through Italy and perhaps visiting Venice but alas, that would have to be enjoyed another time.

I'd visited Italy on my motorbike in 2009 and got the distinct feeling that Italians didn't want me there. Having said that, I didn't speak a work of their language at the time, so much of the blame rested on me. This time I made sure I knew just enough to be polite and order cake and coffee. What more did one need? I also promised myself I'd be super nice, even if this was not reciprocated. If things went wrong, I'd rise above it and walk away; there was to be none of this Mr Angry stuff. I wanted to like Italy and was going to try my hardest to get on with everyone.

After a solid eight-hour sleep, I woke feeling fresh and ready. The anticipation of being about to step foot in a new country filled me with excitement and I was confident about enjoying Italy even though I'd need to zoom through on the fast roads.

I wandered around the ferry and bought myself a breakfast and large coffee, then tidied up my bed and got my stuff ready. As the ferry pulled into the port, I started to feel the familiar desire to rush. I was hoping, as there were so few people on board, that I wouldn't get such feelings but it was worse than ever. Usually, I can follow the crowd but this time there was no crowd to follow, I had to work it out for myself. I found some stairs and waited for the barrier to be removed.

I could feel my heart racing away but there was nothing I could do about it so I listened to the huge metal-on-metal clocks resonating around the ferry as it docked. A few minutes later a young lady took the barrier away and looked over at me.

'Are you okay?' she asked, with a thick Italian accent.

This threw me as I thought, from the outside, I looked fine. Perhaps my stupid anxieties were showing through.

'I'm fine, just a little nervous of Italian people,' I said, smiling.

She laughed and hit me gently on the back, pushing me towards the steps. When I reached the bottom, the door I thought I had to go through was closed and locked. I went back up one flight where I found a door to the deck. I walked through and was surprised to see lots of lorries and trucks. I have no idea where the people driving them had stayed as the ferry had felt pretty much empty. I looked around for my bike but couldn't find it.

'Bloody hell, can't you get anything right?'

I was obviously at the wrong end of the ferry so made my way to the front and *voila*! There was my beautiful bike, waiting patiently for her daddy.

Just as I was about to switch on my GPS the doors started opening. My heart rate was nice and slow, and I felt no signs of panic. This was surprising, as behind me were a load of lorries and they're dab hands at these crossings. I thought this over as the lorries followed me into Italy. The route into Brindisi was easy and I didn't make a mistake. I did feel a slight sense of relief though when the lorries drove past as I stopped to examine the map. The plan was to ride up the SS379, then the SS16 to Bari, then to switch to the A14 until its end near Chieti. Once there I'd re-examine the map and decide what to do.

The SS379 and SS16 was just what I was expecting. There was an element of beauty, an element of seaside and an element of Italian madness. Just after Bari, I switched to the toll road which was further away from the sea and much faster. The Italian element seemed to disappear, but I had a great view of the surrounding countryside which was just begging to be explored.

With my fuel gauge reading zero I spotted a petrol station and pulled in. Before filling up with Super Unleaded I glanced down at the Italian cheat sheet I'd fixed to the top of my tank bag. When I went in to pay, I used a few of my Italian words and smiled a lot. The chap serving me seemed to appreciate it and smiled back. I know it probably seems like a tiny thing to most people but to me it was a big deal. Perhaps I was going to be accepted by the Italians after all.

I made good progress on the fast toll roads but had to stop a few times to hand money over at the booths. One instance in particular stood out. As I approached, I looked for a manned booth but there were none. No problem. I chose a booth and rode in, stopping nice and close to the machine. When I inserted my ticket I was told it was 37 Euros.

'Bloody hell!' I said, swallowing hard.

I was about to extract my credit card when a car came zooming up behind me and stopped not a foot from my back wheel. There's nothing quite like a bit of pressure to get those emotional juices flowing but I ignored it and inserted my card into the machine. I was trying to read the small screen in the sunshine when the car behind me beeped her horn and shouted something out of the window. I imagined the rough translation to be something like 'will you get a bloody move on'. I raised my hand in a 'sorry, I'm doing my best here' kind of way. She didn't appreciate this and beeped at me again, waving her fist.

Mr Angry stomped into the room but was aware that he had to behave. I typed my pin number into the machine and waited for a receipt but got nothing. I could hear the lady in the car behind shouting, which pissed me off even more. I pressed the red help button.

'Can I have a receipt please?'

'The ticket is your receipt,' came the reply.

I told him that the ticket was still in the machine. This time he shouted.

'THE TICKET IS YOUR RECEIPT!'

The lady behind moved her car up to my back wheel and nudged me, causing me to almost drop my bike. This was now going down a route that I'd promised myself I wouldn't go down.

I thanked the obnoxious machine man for his help, tapped my gear lever and rode away without my receipt. Once I'd calmed down, I thought about my performance and congratulated myself on doing the right thing. Perhaps boring old Mr Calm can contain Mr Angry after all, or perhaps Mr Angry is a little more aware of his surroundings than Mr Calm originally gave him credit for.

As I chugged towards Rome my brain began to wander. Why did I not feel panicky when I left the ferry in Brindisi? I remembered getting a bit uptight when I went too far down the staircase. I then got a little more uptight when I found myself at the wrong end of the ferry. I could feel Mr Angry edging ever closer to making an appearance; the shield around me was getting stronger. When the doors to the ferry started opening, I remembered the feeling of not being particularly concerned that a load of experienced lorry drivers were following me out of the ferry. In fact, I almost revelled in the challenge.

I thought this over and came to my conclusion: it was the elements that came with Mr Angry that stopped me from getting anxious. The combination of not really caring what other people thought and a large dollop of confidence made all the difference. Would life be better if I had these elements all the time? What would I be like? These thoughts went round and round until I worked it out. As a person, I'd lose more than I gained. It's the stupid little idiot that people love! I'd be normal and where's the fun in that?

I rode around Rome's ring road and headed north for a while until my backside felt like it was about to fall off. My right knee had gone through a bit painful, then through really bloody painful, and was now crying out for me to stop. I asked my GPS to locate a campsite and threatened it with complete destruction should it fail.

Half an hour later I arrived at a campsite and it looked good. I rode to reception, booked a place and followed the lady to a nice quiet area. It was perfect. It's a wonderful feeling arriving at a site after a hard day in the seat. Before unpacking and preparing my camp for the night, I walked around allowing my joints to refill with fluid and my backside to return to something that resembled a backside.

Fifteen minutes later my body had all but recovered.

After a long shower, I went to reception to find out where to get hot food. My word was I in for a treat! It turned out they had a superb chef and quite a repertoire of excellent dishes. I hadn't booked, which meant there was nowhere for them to put me. But they soon sorted that out with a table of my very own from the owner's house. I placed my order and enjoyed the moment as I sat there indulging in a fine Chianti.

When my starter arrived, beef tagliatelle, it looked and smelt divine. It was also huge which worried me a little. As I munched my way through, I kept promising I would stop and allow space for my main course but before I knew it, my plate was empty.

Luckily, my main course of pork and bacon in a red wine sauce was far smaller than my starter, which suited me perfectly. I made my way through it, concentrating on the wonderful flavours. It really was sublime and not what I was expecting at all.

When dessert arrived, I just looked at it for a while. It was a not insubstantial piece of rich crème caramel badness and sitting next to it was a decent-sized jug full of melted chocolate waiting to be drizzled all over the top. I was really starting to like Italy.

After my incredible meal I returned to my tent, made myself a strong coffee and wrote my blog. I'd managed to polish off a whole bottle of Chianti that evening and was feeling quite tired, so I kept the blog short and climbed into my sleeping bag.

I woke a couple of hours later with a very itchy head. Then my arm felt itchy. Then I could have sworn something ran up my neck and over my face. I grabbed my torch and switched it on.

'Oh Christ!'

The tent walls were alive with hundreds and hundreds of giant ants—and they were all over me too. I jumped up and vacated my tent as quickly as I could. I stripped off in the dark, brushed myself down and spent a few minutes running my fingers through my hair.

Once I was happy, I was ant-free, I re-evaluated the situation. I was standing, completely naked, next to a tent full of giant ants in the middle of a campsite in the middle of the night. And on top of all that, I had a headache from hell from all the wine.

I let out a big sigh, shook the hell out of my boxers and put them back on. I shone the torch inside the tent and took a look. It really was heaving with ants. I quickly grabbed my water bottle and devised a plan.

First, I needed to empty the tent. Some of the bags were close to the entrance so getting them out was easy. The rest were right at the back which wasn't so nice, but without any other choices I just got on with it. With all my stuff removed I hunted through it all for some headache tablets.

I wasn't sure how to get the ants out of the tent, but I was sure of one thing—the tent would need to be moved. I picked it up and plonked it down about 20ft away. When I returned to the original spot, I was horrified to discover the ground alive with ants and right in the middle of where I'd pitched it was a large two-inch diameter hole that led down into their nest. I shuddered as I watched them busily scurrying around. Horrible.

I took the poles out of my tent, turned it inside out and shook the living daylights out of it. Then I turned it the right way around and shook it some more. This got rid of most of the ants, so I moved to another location and did the same again, and again, and again. When I was sure all the ants were gone, I reinstalled the poles and found another spot to camp—first checking the ground for ants, holes and any other creepy crawlies. Then I went through the same routine with my stuff; shaking it, examining it and shaking it more.

When I finally climbed into my sleeping bag it was almost four. I closed my eyes and hoped for sleep, but images of my tent walls covered in ants persisted in my mind. I switched the torch on and checked. All clear. I did eventually manage to get some sleep but suffice to say it wasn't great.

My route had taken me from Brindisi, up the coast road to Bari, through Andria, Foggia, Vasto, Chieti and Avezzano. I then went around Rome and found a campsite just to the north.

Mileage was 424 miles, bringing the total for the trip to 4,762 miles.

DAY THIRTY

SUNDAY, 16TH JULY 2017

What's A Little Bit Of Spittle Between Friends?

WHEN I woke up, I was pleased to see the tent ant-free. I dragged my sore body out of the tent feeling quite sorry for myself. After a strong coffee, I packed up and examined the map. I set Grenoble into the GPS which gave me a distance of 530 miles and seemed like a good number to aim for. The route took me up the E35 through Orvieto, Fabro and Montevarchi, then around Florence to Bologna, Modena, Parma, Placenza, Asti, Turin and into France. From there I'd head to Grenoble and keep an eye out for a campsite.

That kind of distance would be a challenge on a good day but after just a few hours' sleep it really was going to be hard. On top of that, I had those feisty Italians to deal with!

Before leaving I checked the bike over quickly and found that the chain could do with a bit of adjustment. I removed my tool roll from my pannier and laid it out. Sitting there tinkering with the bike was a real pleasure and changed the mood from 'morning hardship' to 'another fine day'. It's always the small things.

I rode out of the campsite with a weird confidence. Perhaps it was my new 28-word Italian vocabulary or lack of sleep. Either way, I was looking forward to the day ahead.

All went well for the first few hours. I covered a good distance with no problems. By late morning I was running low on fuel so pulled into a large petrol station. The payment chap seemed nice enough and reciprocated my few words of Italian with a smile. With a new confidence in my ability to get on with Italians, I decided to brave the petrol station shop for food.

When it was my turn, I opened with another 'Buongiorno!' and a smile and pointed to a thing that looked like a Scotch egg. He removed it from the display cabinet and said something in Italian. As he spoke, a large lump of spit flew from his mouth and onto the thing that looked like a Scotch egg. He noticed this and attempted to wipe it off with his dirty apron. Wanting to be polite but not wanting to chow down on another man's spit, I shook my head and pointed to one that hadn't been spat on.

The man then frowned, became very loud and showed how he'd wiped his spit away with his apron. He then put it on the counter and tried to charge me three Euros. I shook my head and pointed again to another one in the display cabinet. He picked up the one he'd spat on and slammed it down, and then held his hand out.

'THREE EURO!'

I smiled politely, about turned and walked to the exit. At this point, he started shouting. My normal response would have been to return and do some shouting of my own (are you telling me that you're not going to charge me extra for that layer of saliva?) but I was trying hard to not have any bad experiences so I kept my mouth closed. By the time I'd got on my bike he was back behind the counter, probably spitting on everyone else's food. I reminded myself that every country has a man like him.

I accelerated up to speed and re-joined the motorway. After a few miles, I spotted a couple of lorries ahead. Now, my bike is not super-fast and anything over about seventy feels like you're about to take off. As such I tend to just sit at seventy and enjoy the ride.

As I got closer, I could see that overtaking the lorries was going to take some time at seventy, so I accelerated up to eighty. When I got close enough, I checked my mirrors and with nothing behind me, I pulled out and started to overtake.

When I next checked my mirrors, I could see the flickering lights of a car's headlights coming up from behind at quite a speed, so I went up to ninety. Before I managed to get past the last lorry, the car drove up to my back wheel and flashed me.

The only option available was to continue overtaking the last lorry, then move back into the slow lane. This was obviously not good enough for the car driver, who continued flashing and got even closer to my back wheel. I had no idea what he wanted me to do. Unfortunately for him, I was unable to spontaneously vaporise myself and the bike into thin air.

Once in front of the lorries, I slowed back down and felt miserable. I so wanted to like Italy but some of its people were making it incredibly hard. I hoped it would end on a good note.

A hundred or so miles later I came up behind another lorry and a coach. With nothing behind me, I accelerated to eighty and started overtaking them. When I spotted some lights behind me, I quickly slowed and slipped back in behind the lorry.

The driver in the approaching car saw this and flashed to let me go. I thanked him, pulled out and zipped up to ninety, and the car kept a reasonable distance. When I slipped in front of the coach, the car behind came up beside me. It was a beautiful gleaming black Ferrari 599 GT. The chap pointed to the bike, grinned like an idiot and stuck his thumb up. He then floored it and disappeared like a bat out of hell. The sound it made up close was incredible. He was having some serious fun. Good man!

I didn't get to see much of Italy but from what I saw from the road, the coast looked very nice as did the central mountainous regions. However, it was the approach to the Alps that did it for me. I turned left and whizzed into France before I got there but seeing those majestic mountains come into view was quite spectacular.

My opinion of Italians? Well, they're like normal people but with added spice and passion. I see that as a good thing, but they don't suffer fools gladly and being that I sit firmly in the fool category, I find that a little sad.

I was also not too enamoured by the cost of their toll roads. The first day cost me about 45 Euros in tolls and the second about 90 Euros, but that did include a very long tunnel as I entered France.

That transition is something to be experienced. When I eventually emerged from the long tunnel, I was confronted with the mountains of the French Alps, rich, green countryside and that feeling only France can inspire. The sun was getting lower in the sky and even though my arse was killing me, I just didn't want it to end. There were a number of campsites close by but I picked one about 50 miles away so I could continue riding for longer.

By the time I reached it, my backside was about ready to fall off and my right knee was crying out for me to stop. Reception was closed so I picked a place, parked up and climbed off. It felt so good. I lay flat on the ground and stretched, with my knees straight I could actually feel them returning to normal.

The campsite was about 15 miles southwest of Grenoble. I'd done incredibly well to get there, especially as I'd had bugger all sleep the night before. In all, I'd covered 510 miles; quite an achievement. Unfortunately, what I hadn't done so well was keeping a close eye on my caffeine levels. The last coffee I'd had was in the morning.

Once I'd set up camp, I searched through my panniers for anything containing caffeine. I had a cracking headache, but my panniers were bare. With both my Thermos and jar of instant coffee granules empty, I set off towards the entrance to see if there were any shops but there were none. After nosing around the reception area one of the owners appeared from his home upstairs and asked if he could help me.

'I'd love a large cup of strong coffee.'

He looked at me in a weird kind of way, then shook my hand vigorously.

'We have beer,' he said, grinning.

I explained I had a headache and needed caffeine, but he just repeated that he had beer. It was one of those weird moments where I didn't know if he or I was the weirdo. I asked him again for coffee, but he didn't seem to understand. He stared at me for a moment, then about turned and disappeared upstairs. I waited around thinking he was going to come back with a coffee, but he didn't. I returned to my bike and went through all my bags hoping against hope I'd missed something.

In my dirty washing bag, I found a warm bottle of flat Coke Zero. The combination of the Coke Zero, lots of water and a few tablets dulled the headache but I couldn't budge it completely without coffee.

I asked a few of my neighbours if there was anywhere close by selling food or coffee but I was completely out of luck. Incredibly, no one had any coffee either. On the plus side, while going through all my luggage, I found a family-sized pack of onion ring crisps. At least I wasn't going to starve. In complete contrast to the night before, my evening was spent eating crisps that stank of cheesy feet and writing my blog. This would never have happened in Italy.

My route had taken me from my campsite just north of Rome, up the E35 through Orvieto, Fabro and Montevarchi, then around Florence to Bologna, Modena, Parma, Placenza, Asti, Turin and into France. From there I went around Grenoble and finally settled into a campsite about 15 miles to the southwest.

Mileage was 510 miles bringing the total for the trip to 5,272 miles.

DAY THIRTY-ONE

The Wonders Of France

THE LACK of caffeine caused the headache to last all night. It got progressively worse until, at about six, I decided to get up. I packed my camp away and left the site within 45 minutes.

My priority was to find somewhere selling coffee. Every bump or cat's eye or manhole cover caused even more pain in my already fragile head. Luckily, I found a petrol station not far up the road. I bought three double espressos and downed them with a litre of water.

I pushed the bike over to the corner and looked at the map. After working out routes, I decided to simply set the GPS to avoid main roads and tolls and asked it to take me to Nancy, about 350 miles away. I checked the route it came up with on the map and it certainly looked interesting. By the time I left, about 15 minutes later, my headache had gone completely.

The first couple of hours were spent meandering my way north on the windy roads of the western edge of the French Alps. The GPS made a few interesting choices; one included trying to route me through a tunnel that was closed. In fact, it looked like it was only partially built. Another interesting choice was when it tried to detour me through a large lake. I know the Transalp is a tough little cookie but riding through water more than 100ft deep was simply asking too much, even for a Honda. Perhaps if it was a BMW...

As the day progressed the scenery changed from snow-capped mountains to rolling fields. I love the mountains, but the rolling fields of France have a draw of their own which is equally as enjoyable. I contently chugged ever northwards enjoying the small roads and villages as I went. I stopped in a delightful place called Dole for a huge slice of pizza, some cake and two double espressos. Afterwards I walked around the town and took some photographs.

With the sun not far off the horizon, I finally pulled into a campsite at about eight. Reception was closed so I rode around and found a spot at the back next to a small stream. As I climbed off the bike, my stomach rumbled in a way that made me most uncomfortable—if you know what I mean.

I unpacked, changed and set up camp. By this time my stomach was cramping, and I was in dire need of a toilet. Unfortunately, my ideal spot by the stream meant I had to walk past just about every pitch in the site to get to the toilet block. Normally this would not have been a problem, but everyone was sitting outside, deliberately, to watch me as I walked by. As such I felt unable to run to the toilet while shouting 'IT'S AN EMERGENCY! GET OUT OF THE WAY!'

Instead, I clenched my buttocks so tightly it would have taken a vice to prise them apart and walked (from the knees down) as if I didn't need to visit the lavatory at all. When I reached the block, I zipped inside and looked around for the toilets. I found showers, sinks, nappy changing facilities and even a stock cupboard... but no toilets. Then I spotted the familiar sign but to my horror, the door was locked and needed a code to open. No doubt the code was given to campers by reception.

'Oh shit.'

I tried a few numbers to no avail, then walked (from the knees down) back to my tent, where I dug out my supply of Imodium and ate them all.

The game was on. Who would win? Would it be the contents of my stomach, desperate to escape or the power of Imodium? I decided to wait and see but after another rumble, I changed my mind. It was time to break the door down. I walk-skip-jumped past happy campers and I tried a few more numbers on the keypad but to no avail. I pushed the door a little with my shoulder, but it was not going to budge.

There was only one option left. I shuffled up to the closest, irritatingly happy campers.

'Où sont les toilettes?' I said, trying my hardest to keep my face from looking stressed or in need.

They all pointed to the locked door.

'Deux, trois, quatre, cinq, six.'

Not being a native, it took me a while to work it out. The instant I had, I started towards the toilet. And that's when the questions started.

'You must be the biker. Are you travelling alone?'

'So, tell us about your trip.'

'Did you like Romania?'

'That's a huge bike. How do you manage?'

I tried to be polite but the conversation combined with 'battle of the buttocks' was zapping my energy and patience. I made my excuses and left. When I reached the coded door, I actually said a little prayer to the flying spaghetti monster. I typed in the numbers and pulled the handle down. It was like opening the door to a giant treasure chest though instead of gold coins and diamonds there were beautiful toilets with toilet paper and soap and everything. I picked the cubicle nearest the wall and took position.

I wasn't completely sure if it was just going to be a windy day or if Krakatoa was going to erupt but, if I was a betting man, I'd have gone for the latter. It turned out to be a windy day.

As I sat on my ceramic throne, I thought about the family who'd given me the number. Were they wondering how it was going? I thought about the people I'd walked past. Were they also wondering how I was getting on?

Why do I do this? Is it just me or is it an English thing? It's bizarre really; if it was a wee, it would be completely fine but as its a number two (I can't even say it), it's all a big secret. I hope I haven't offended anyone.

When I returned from the toilet, I sat on the ground in front of my tent and wrote my blog. Every once in a while, I started laughing and noticed people looking at me. I wondered if they were looking because I was laughing or because they knew I'd just had an emergency poo.

I still had about 230 miles to go before reaching Dieppe. I booked my ferry ticket for six the following evening and hoped to be home by late the next day. I thought about walking through the door and seeing Flowie and my dog Nelly. With that on my mind, I climbed into my sleeping bag and went to sleep.

My route had taken me from southwest of Grenoble through Chapareillan, Seloge, Le Bourget-du-Lac to a closed tunnel. I went back to Le Bourget-du-Lac and continued through La Motte-Servolex, Villard Marin, Saint-Sulpice, Novalaise, Sainte-Marie-d'Alvey, Saint-Didier-de-la-Tour, Saint-Benoît, Les Granges, Druillat, Dole, Gray, Chassigny and finally to my campsite around ten miles north of Nancy.

Mileage was 336 miles, bringing the total for the trip to 5,608 miles.

DAY THIRTY-TWO

The Worry Of Returning Home

I WOKE AT about six to the sound of birdsong and trickling water from the nearby stream. I concentrated hard to keep thoughts of work and problems out of my mind for just one more day, but my mind was worrying about everything.

Why are my sales so bad? Do I still have an income? Have I run out of stock? Is my bank account still alive? I forced my mind to return to the present and got up. I had 230 miles to Dieppe and the last day is often the most dangerous. The mind wanders and concentration ebbs away and the next thing you know, you're on your arse sliding down the road at sixty.

I grabbed my bag and made my way to the toilet block. I smiled as I walked past the locked and coded toilet door; with the amount of Imodium I'd eaten, having a poo this side of Christmas would probably be a physical impossibility.

I entered the shower cubicle, then stood at the sink and shaved the last few days of scrub from my face. This is when the coughing started. It sounded like a heavy smoker coughing up yesterday's lining. It was absolutely disgusting, and it went on, and on, and on... hawking, coughing, spitting.

I finished up and left expecting to see a large man in his fifties or sixties leaning on the sink struggling for breath. Instead I saw a slim woman, probably in her early thirties with a fag in hand. She had an angry look on her face and hawked up again as I walked by. I relaxed when I was no longer in spitting distance.

Within half an hour my stuff was packed, and the bike was ready to go. I grabbed a piece of notepaper and went to reception which was still closed. The board outside told me the price. I folded up a ten Euro and posted it under the door with a note to the owner.

The first half of the trip went well. I stopped for petrol and food a couple of times but made one mistake around the halfway mark and had to do a little creative riding to avoid getting sucked onto a toll road. I stopped and looked at a policeman who was watching me. I shrugged and pointed to the grass verge. He gestured in a way which I took to mean 'You're English, so we both know you're going to do exactly as you please anyway'. I agreed and rode over the grass verge and down the other side. Thinking it was only right to say thanks, I shouted 'Bonjour Monsieur!', then promptly realised I'd said hello sir instead of thanks or goodbye. I looked in my mirror and saw him waving as I rode away.

In Dieppe, I found a nice restaurant. As I always do in Dieppe at the end of a long journey, I ordered moules marinière with cream, garlic and parsley. It felt good sitting there in the port, almost home. I was tempted to have a glass of wine but when you're trying to get a heavy bike onto a ferry you need to have balance on your side, so I decided against it.

At the ferry terminal I checked in and waited to board. I had almost two hours to kill and did my best to fend off worrying about what I'd find when I got home. Unfortunately, I lost the battle and checked my emails. All of a sudden, I was in a world of bills, pressure and anxiety and I wondered if I'd done the right thing in going away for such a long time. *Was it selfish to leave my wife for such a long period of time? A dog's life is relatively short and was it right to leave her for a whole month? Would my business be permanently affected?* I started to regret my trip and wished I've never gone. What had I done?

'Welcome back Richard,' I muttered, miserably.

I decided that food might make time go a little faster so wandered over to the cafeteria and bought a chocolate muffin, a Snickers bar and a delicious thing called a chocochino. I downed the lot and time still went slowly by.

Eventually we were allowed to board, and I made a mental note that I'd entered at the rear, was on the left-hand side.

After two nights of almost no sleep, all it took for me to drift off was a comfortable chair, a set of closed eyes and about 30 seconds. I slept solidly for the four-hour crossing, and for another half an hour for good measure. Luckily, a kind-hearted gentleman saw fit to wake me from my dribbling slumber before the ferry returned to France.

I confidently rode out of the ferry and into the night air of Newhaven. My mind was a mess. I felt exhilarated, exhausted and worried, all at the same time. I was looking forward to seeing Flowie and Nelly immensely, but I was most concerned about what I'd find when I opened my emails.

Before I knew it, I was bouncing up the driveway to our home. Flowie had opened the doors to the garage, so I rode straight in. As I dragged my tired bones off the bike, I was greeted by Nelly who leant against me and pined, refusing to leave my side until she'd had a big long cuddle. I walked into the kitchen to find Flowie smiling, her arms open wide. It was good to be back.

There were a few diversions during the journey so the actual route I took was a bit messier than the list of places I passed through would suggest. From my camp-site north of Nancy, I passed through Vroil, Charmont, Possesse, Vadenay, Bouy, Reims, Soissons, Compiègne, Beauvais, Neufchâtel-en-Bray then finally arrived at Dieppe.

Including the last segment of the trip from Newhaven to back home, I covered 310 miles, bringing the trip total to 5,918 miles.

I booted up my computer and opened Outlook. As I sat there waiting for the vast amount of emails to download, my brain started to wander and soon enough I was back at the port of Dieppe worrying myself senseless and questioning my decision to go away for such a long time.

I recalled watching an elderly couple sitting nearby. They got up and walked over to the toilet. She went in and he waited outside. When she appeared again, I heard him say 'Have you washed your hands dear?'

She went back inside and washed her hands. When she reappeared, she walked straight past him and stood looking around blankly. He walked over and put his hand on her shoulder.

'It's okay Hilda, I'm here. We're on our way home now.'

He gave her a big cuddle. She didn't cuddle him back. Instead her arms hung limply by her sides. He glanced at me and his eyes had filled up.

This was the answer to my question. Was it right to go away for such a long time? Yes, it was.

Life doesn't last forever and it's important to make the most of it. I hope Hilda and her husband make the most of theirs.

ABOUT THE AUTHOR

RICHARD LIVES in a small village in East Sussex with his wife Flowie, Newfoundland dog Nelly and two cats, Frodo and Kiri.

He came to biking rather late in life, after watching an episode of Long Way Down.

A career change from computer chap to business owner allowed him a freedom he uses to indulge in his two passions: being an idiot and writing about it.

Long may it last.